Hawaii on Foot

by Frances Carter

Bess Press, Inc.
P. O. Box 22388
Honolulu, HI 96822

To Steve,
my welcome companion on many of these walks

THE BESS PRESS, P. O. Box 22388, Honolulu, HI 96822

Library of Congress
Catalog Card No.: 89-81823
Carter, Frances
  Hawaii on Foot
Honolulu, Hawaii: Bess Press, Inc.
96 pages

ISBN: 0-935848-81-9

Cover design: Z. Leimalama Harris

Editing and typesetting: Revé Shapard

TABLE OF CONTENTS

Symbols:

 Beach and Park Walks

 Historic Walks

 Nature Walks

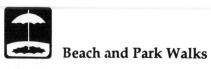 **General Walks**

INTRODUCTION

Hawaii is a wonderful state to explore on foot. The mild climate and lovely scenery make it an ideal place to get out of the car or tour bus and take a closer look at the features which make Hawaii very special to those of us who live here. You'll find intriguing flora and fauna, fascinating historical sites, unusual geological formations and much more.

This is not a hiking book. Hiking books usually focus on wilderness areas, and involve strenuous exertion. The walks presented here are appropriate for people of all ages who like to walk. Although we do include some nature walks, we also offer a variety of other types of areas which are great for walking.

Some of the places we've included offer guided walks. Whenever possible, try to take advantage of these because they offer a fun way to learn more about an area from really knowledgeable people.

We've also included a resource list of all the guided walks and walking programs we could find in the islands. If you have more for us, or other suggestions, please write to us at Bess Press, P. O. Box 22388, Honolulu, HI 96822. Have fun!

FC

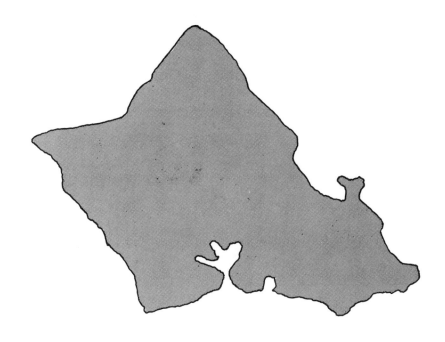

Island of Oahu

Waikiki

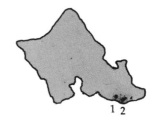

1 2

WALK 1 - WAIKIKI

1.25 miles, one way
30-45 minutes

This walk begins at **King's Village** on Kaiulani Street, just off Kalakaua. This quaint shopping complex was built in 1971 with a turn-of-the-century British theme. Every evening at 6:15 there is a "changing of the Guards" ceremony with guards dressed in uniforms that are reproductions of those worn by the Hawaiian Royal Guards during Kalakaua's reign. In the center courtyard, you'll find "Celebrity Circle," with handprints of famous people.

Walk toward the ocean on Kaiulani Street and turn right on Kalakaua. This avenue, named for King David Kalakaua, has been the main road into Waikiki since the 1860s.

On the corner of Kalakaua and Lewers is the **First Hawaiian Bank**, which contains beautiful murals by Jean Charlot. Located above the tellers' area, the murals represent Hawaiian history from the time of Captain Cook's arrival to the arrival of the missionaries.

Turn down Lewers, walking toward the ocean to Kalia Road, then turn right and walk until you come to **Fort DeRussy**. This property was acquired by the U. S. government in 1904, and was named Fort DeRussy in 1909 in honor of Brigadier General Rene DeRussy. The building that now houses the **U.S. Army Museum**, Battery Randolph, was built as a coastal artillery battery in 1911.

The Museum has an interesting collection of military memorabilia and is worth a visit if you have the time. There is no admission charge, and the museum is open daily except

11

Monday from 10:00 a.m. to 4:30 p.m.

Upstairs is a new Regional Visitor Center provided by the U.S. Army Corps of Engineers. The Center contains a free, multi-media show of Pacific life. It has the same hours as the museum.

Continue on along Kalia Road to the **Hilton Hawaiian Village** complex. The Hilton's Rainbow Tower has two stunning 286-foot tall ceramic tile murals, one facing the ocean and one facing the street. The murals were created in 1968 by Millard Sheets, and at the time were the tallest murals in the world. Each contains over 8,000 tiles.

The Hilton grounds contain an impressive assortment of swimming pools, waterfalls, plants and even a mini zoo including tropical penguins, African flamingos, carp and a variety of exotic birds. At 9:00 a.m. and 4:00 p.m., you can watch the penguins being fed.

For a Guided Walk in this area, see Walk 1, page 93.

 **WALK 2 - WAIKIKI BEACH**   1.5 miles
45 minutes

This walk is on the beach, so dress appropriately and protect yourself from too much sun. (Read WALK 1 for more information about many of the places you'll pass along the beach.)

Begin behind the Hilton Hawaiian Village at the **Duke Kahanamoku Lagoon**. The lagoon was named for Hawaii's most famous swimmer, Duke Paoa Kahanamoku, who won gold medals in the Olympics of 1912 and 1920.

Conrad Hilton purchased this property in 1956 and built the Hilton Hawaiian Village.

Walking toward Diamond Head, the next beach you'll come to is **Fort DeRussy Beach**. This property has been owned by the U.S. Government since 1904, and is the site of the Hale Koa, a military hotel. Next door is Battery Randolph, which houses the U.S. Army Museum and the Army Corps of Engineers' Regional Visitor Center, free attractions which are both worth a visit. They are both open daily from 10:00 a.m. to 4:30 p.m.

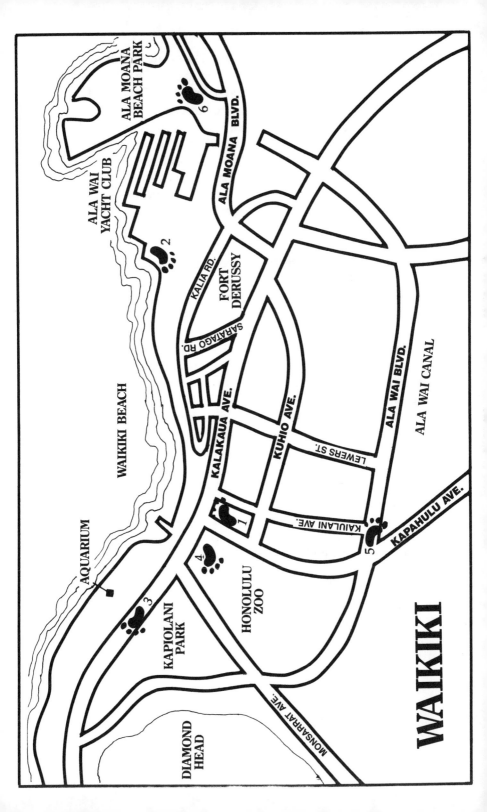

A little farther along the beach is the **Halekulani Hotel,** which has long been a Waikiki landmark. The hotel was originally built in 1931 and renovated in 1983. Today only the main building is left from the original structure.

Pass the Sheraton, and pause to admire the famous **Royal Hawaiian Hotel,** which opened in 1927 and became known as the "Pink Palace." This elegant old hotel has been in danger of demolition several times, but fortunately has survived.

Continue walking until you come to the colonial-style **Sheraton Moana Surfrider,** which is Waikiki's oldest surviving hotel. The Moana recently underwent a $50 million renovation to restore her to the beauty which gave her the name of "First Lady of Waikiki." The hotel first opened in 1901, and is listed on the National Register of Historic Places.

This is a pleasant place to stop for a cool drink in the outdoor bar under the huge banyan tree, which is over 100 years old. From this site Robert Louis Stevenson began the tale *Treasure Island.* From here also was broadcast the radio show "Hawaii Calls." This classy hotel was originally owned by the Matson Navigation Company, and was a favorite among those who visited Hawaii by steamboat.

Past the Moana and near the sidewalk on Kalakaua, you'll find the **Kahuna Stones.** The stones have a plaque that recounts the legend of four kahunas (priests) who arrived in Hawaii from Tahiti in about the 14th century. It is said that upon departing from Hawaii, the kahunas transferred their power to these rocks.

At the end of Kapahulu, you'll pass **Kuhio Beach Park,** which was named for Kalakaua's nephew Prince Kuhio Kalanianaole, who once had a home here near the large banyan tree.

Kapahulu Avenue marks the end of Waikiki. It's about 11/2 miles to this point. The wall that extends out into the water is a good place to watch the boogie boarders.

You can continue walking along the beach about another 1/2 mile, all the way to the **Waikiki Aquarium,** another attraction worth a visit. (See WALK 3).

WALK 3 - KAPIOLANI PARK   2.2 miles
(Kalakaua Avenue at Monsarrat)   1 hour

The trail around the park covers 1.8 miles. If you include the perimeter of the Zoo, the walk is 2.2 miles. There are restroom facilities and plenty of places to stop along the way for a picnic or to enjoy the scenery. This area is usually warm and sunny, so protect yourself from getting too much sun.

This 170-acre park was named after Queen Kapiolani, and was dedicated in 1877 as Honolulu's first large public park. The park contains a softball diamond, driving range, archery range, tennis courts, an exercise station, an amphitheater and a bandstand where free performances are frequently held.

A good place to start is on Kalakaua near the tennis courts. You'll see "Jogger's Rest," a Victorian trolley shelter that was installed in 1904 by the Honolulu Rapid Transit company. Their electric trolley brought people to the Aquarium, which was then considered to be a long way out of town.

Walking toward Diamond Head, you can cross Kalakaua Avenue and tour the **Waikiki Aquarium** along the way or save it for another day. The Aquarium is open daily from 9:00 a.m. to 5:00 p.m., and requests a $2.50 admission donation. It's well worth the small admission price to see the excellent displays, which include chambered nautilus, live corals, and the Humuhumunukunukuapua'a, Hawaii's State Fish.

Next door to the Aquarium is the **Natatorium**, a war memorial built in 1927 honoring Hawaii's soldiers who died in World War I. At that time it was the country's largest saltwater swimming pool. The 100-meter pool was designed for Olympic swimming meets and public swimming, but is now closed due to deterioration. A "Save the Natatorium" group has been raising money to restore the memorial.

Continuing toward Diamond Head along Kalakaua, you'll see the **Dillingham Fountain** in the center of Kalakaua. The fountain was dedicated to Louise Dillingham, wife of one of Honolulu's prominent businessmen.

Continue on around the road, turning left at Paki. You'll pass the Archery Range on your right and the Driving Range on your left.

At the corner of Monsarrat you can decide if you want to

include the perimeter of the **Zoo** (WALK 4). If so, go straight and turn left at Kapahulu and walk back toward Kalakaua where you started. Otherwise, turn left at Monsarrat and walk toward Kalakaua.

On Monsarrat you'll see the entrance to the **Waikiki Shell**, which was built in 1953. The Shell seats over 8,000 people and has been used for all types of performances as well as commencement ceremonies.

The **Kodak Hula Show** is held near the Shell at 10:00 a.m., Tuesday through Thursday. Presented since 1937, it is the longest-running show in Hawaii. Admission is $2.50 for adults, free for children 12 and under.

If you're making this walk on Saturday or Sunday, you might want to cross over and walk along the Zoo's fence, where you'll see the works of local artists displayed at the Weekend Art Mart from 10:00 a.m. to 4:00 p.m.

Continue on toward Kalakaua, which will take you back to where you started.

For Guided Walks in this area, see Walks 1 and 2, page 93.

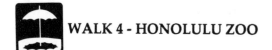 WALK 4 - HONOLULU ZOO   1 mile
                                              30-45 minutes

The Zoo is a great place to walk with small children. There is plenty for them to look at, and the walking distance isn't too tiring. There is a $1.00 admission for adults, but children under 12 are free.

The Zoo is open daily from 8:30 a.m. to 4:30 p.m. At the entrance, ask for a map, which will show you the layout of the Zoo and the locations of specific exhibits.

Kids will especially enjoy the Petting Zoo and the elephant demonstrations. On Saturdays from 10:30 a.m. to noon at the Education Pavilion, the Zoo presents "Animal Tails."

The Zoo is small and you can walk around the whole park in half an hour, but it's a great place to linger, watch the animal antics or have a picnic.

During the summer, you can visit the Zoo for free on Wednesdays and enjoy an outdoor performance on the center stage. They call it the "Wildest Show in Town." Gates open at 4:30 p.m. and the performance is around 6:30 p.m.

WALK 5 - ALA WAI CANAL

2.5 miles, one way
45 minutes

Waikiki used to be filled with taro fields, fish ponds and rice fields, but by 1900 businessmen saw the ponds and fields as obstacles to Waikiki's development. Construction of the Ala Wai Canal began in 1921. Coral was removed from the canal and used to fill in the fields and ponds in Waikiki.

You can start this walk anywhere along the Ala Wai depending on how far you'd like to walk. The canal is about 2.9 miles long and runs the length of Waikiki. On the mountain side is the **Ala Wai Golf Course**. Late afternoon or early morning is a good time to walk along the canal since it is hot during midday. In the afternoon you can watch the canoe paddlers practicing in their outrigger canoes.

After you cross Kalakaua Avenue, the Ala Wai curves toward the ocean, and there is a lovely promenade bordered by Chinese banyan trees on both sides of the canal. This walkway ends at Ala Moana Boulevard and the **Ala Wai Yacht Harbor**.

If you want to explore the Yacht Harbor, go up the stairway at the end of the walkway. If you turn left and walk to Hobron Lane and turn right, this will take you to the boats. The **Ilikai Hotel** is a pleasant place to take a rest and watch the sunset at their outdoor bar, which overlooks the Yacht Harbor. Or if you turn right on Ala Moana Boulevard and cross over at the crosswalk to Ala Moana Park, you can walk along the end of the Yacht Harbor. From here you can watch the boats as they sail out of the Harbor.

WALK 6 - ALA MOANA PARK AND BEACH
(Ala Moana Blvd. across from Ala Moana Shopping Center)

3 miles
30-45 minutes

This is a favorite beach park of many Honolulu residents. This 76-acre park contains picnic facilities, a walking and jogging trail, tennis courts, snack bars, an outdoor gym and a safe swimming area.

The trail around the park covers 2 miles. If you include Magic Island, the peninsula jutting out beyond the parking lot, the walk is 3 miles.

The Diamond Head end of the park borders the Ala Wai Yacht Harbor, a good spot to watch outrigger canoe paddlers practice in the late afternoon or sailors race their boats on Friday around 5:30 p.m.

The marina was constructed after the Ala Wai Canal was finished in the 1920s. Today it is home to over 700 sailboats and two yacht clubs.

Ala Moana is also a good spot to walk along the beach if you like walking in the sand. The distance from the parking lot to the other end and back is a little over a mile.

The swimming area is an old boat channel that was cut to join Kewalo Basin with the Ala Wai Canal, but was closed off by the construction of Magic Island.

The Kuan Yin Temple (170 N. Vineyard) has one of the loveliest shrines in town.

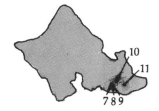

Honolulu

 WALK 7- CHINATOWN

1.25 miles
3-4 hours

Chinatown is one of Honolulu's most historic and fascinating neighborhoods. It offers visitors an opportunity to sample *dim sum*, make an offering to the gods, view an art exhibit or consult an herbalist, all within a fifteen-block area.

No one is sure of the exact date of the arrival of the Chinese in Hawaii, but it is known that Chinese sailors did reach the islands in 1788, and stayed in port for several months. Local historians have decided that 1789 should be commemorated as the official date of the arrival of the Chinese in Hawaii.

The Chinese were the first contract laborers to arrive in the islands. In 1892, Captain John Cass of the British ship *Thetis* brought the first Chinese men under contract for five years at $3.00 per month to work on the plantations.

The Chinese were very enterprising, and when their contracts were up many of them went into business for themselves in the area of town that became known as Chinatown.

In 1886 calamity struck Chinatown when a fire raged out of control, taking the homes of 7,000 Chinese and 350 Hawaiians. The fire lasted three days and destroyed over eight blocks of Chinatown.

Homes and businesses were rebuilt, only to be destroyed in an even greater fire in 1900, which devastated over thirty-eight acres of Chinatown.

Fortunately, the spirit of Chinatown has persisted, and today there is a renaissance in progress that is bringing new life into this special neighborhood.

Chinatown really deserves about half a day for leisurely exploring, but if time doesn't permit, read through and pick out the places you'd like to see first. It's a good idea to start the walk before eating, since there are many exotic delicacies to try along the way. A good place to start is **1. Oahu Market**, corner of King and Kekaulike Streets. A visit to the Oahu Market, founded in 1904, provides a feast for the senses. You'll find Hawaiian, Filipino, Japanese, Korean, and Chinese specialties.

Local fruits are good items for sampling. Try star fruit, mountain apple, lychee and mango. The Chinese were responsible for introducing many of Hawaii's fruits and vegetables, such as lychee, kumquats, persimmons, pomelo, star fruit, apple-banana, and bamboo.

Browse through the hogs' heads, cows' tongues, poi, smoked duck, limu and lomi lomi salmon, and sample whatever you dare. The market is also a good place to buy local flowers inexpensively.

The next four stops are all on King Street. **2. Sun Wah Trading,** 170 North King, has a very large selection of Chinese porcelain, including teapots, cups, bowls, figurines, plates and vases. You can buy rice bowls for as little as 70 cents. **3. Ba-Le**, 150 North King, reportedly has the best French bread in Honolulu, and must surely be the cheapest at three small loaves for $1.00. The owner, Thanh Quuc Lam, turns out 1,400 to 1,600 loaves a day, which he also uses for hefty and inexpensive sandwiches.

Ba-Le also features a Vietnamese-style manapua (steamed bun), which is made with milk and stuffed with mushrooms,

Chinatown

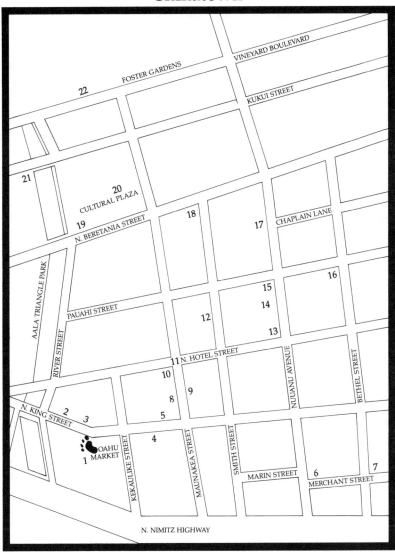

1. Oahu Market
2. Sun Wah Trading
3. Ba-Le
4. Ting Yin Chop Suey
5. Thailand Pacific
6. Royal Saloon Building
7. Kamehameha V Post Office Building
8. Fook Sau Tong
9. Shung Chong Yuein
10. Wo Fat
11. Hotel Street
12. Ramsay ChinatownGallery
13. Encore Saloon Building
14. Lai Fong
15. Pauahi Nuuanu Gallery
16. Hawaii Theatre
17. Pegge Hopper Gallery
18. Sweetheart's Lei Shop
19. Sun Yat-sen Statue
20. Chinatown Cultural Plaza
21. Izumo Taisha Shrine
22. Kuan Yin Temple

carrots, onions, peas, chicken, pork and egg.

The owner says the Ba-Le name is famous in his country, "like McDonald's," and means "Paris" in Vietnamese.

4. Ting Yin Chop Suey, 125 North King, is a favorite stop for *dim sum*, plump rice flour rolls stuffed with meat. Gaze through the window at the trays filled with different types of dim sum and manapua. The brown manapua is baked and usually contains pork. The white one with the red stamp on top is steamed and contains a sweet, black bean paste.

5. Thailand Pacific, 108 North King, calls itself "an exotic Asian Market." It offers an interesting assortment of imports from Thailand, including clothing, jewelry, brass, Thai condiments, canned items, music cassettes and even videotapes in Thai.

Continue walking toward Waikiki on King Street until you get to Nuuanu. Turn right, go one block, and turn left on Merchant. **6. Royal Saloon Building**, is at the corner of Nuuanu and Merchant. This quaint brick building that now contains Murphy's Bar & Grill originally housed the Royal Saloon, which opened in 1890 and was patronized by everyone from stevedores to King Kalakaua. The old saloon served the waterfront for several decades, and today Murphy's carries on the tradition of this memorial to Honolulu's boisterous 19th century waterfront. The street in front of Murphy's is now the site of frequent Friday evening block parties sponsored by the downtown merchants.

7. Kamehameha V Post Office Building, corner of Merchant and Bethel. Although not considered within the boundaries of Chinatown proper, which ends at Nuuanu, this beautifully restored building is on the National Register of Historic Places, and is worth a visit.

The building was built in 1870 during the reign of Kamehameha V, and was Hawaii's first post office building. It also housed the Hawaiian Gazette's publishing and printing plant, and became a U.S. post office in 1900 when Hawaii became a territory. It continued as Hawaii's main post office until 1922, and now houses state welfare offices.

Next door, the Kamehameha V Alan Davis park is a refreshing spot of green amidst the concrete. The park was a project of Honolulu's Garden Club and Outdoor Circle, and is a memorial to Alan S. Davis' contributions to the downtown area.

The fountain in front, which is dominated by impressive Caribbean royal palms, is made of old granite from China that came in as ballast on ships.

Backtrack to King Street and go back to Maunakea. Turn right and go to **8. Fook Sau Tong,** at 1016 Maunakea. This Chinese herb shop has an unusual window display of dried seahorses, snake skins, bones, dried mushrooms and other mysterious substances.

According to Chinese legend, the first treatise on herbal medicine was written during the reign of the Yellow Emperor, Huang-ti, between 2698 and 2598 B.C.

More than 1,000 kinds of plants, twigs, bark, roots, fungi and mushrooms are found in a well-stocked herb shop. A few remedies (some, unfortunately, using endangered species), are seahorse for neck tumors, gall bladder of the bear or tiger bone for aches and pains, rhinoceros horn for allergies, and licorice to allay thirst and relieve distress in breathing due to colds.

Across the street, **9. Shung Chong Yuein,** 1027 Maunakea, is the friendliest Chinese bakery in town. They offer several tempting goodies such as moon cake, wedding cake (which is more like a cookie than cake), almond cookies and peanut candy. The *gin dui,* a Chinese sweet filled with black bean paste or coconut, is also worth a try. The bakery also sells Chinese tea, canned goods and candied vegetables such as lotus root, carrot and squash.

A printer hand-sets the type for the United Chinese Press.

A shrine inside
Shung Chong Yuein
bakery

Noodle factories
turn out miles of
noodles daily.

10. Wo Fat Restaurant, corner Maunakea and Hotel, dates back to 1882, making it the oldest restaurant in Honolulu. The first building was destroyed in the Chinatown fire of 1886. Wat Ging, the restaurant's founder, rebuilt only to have his restaurant destroyed again in the fire of 1900. He persevered however, and his establishment became one of Hawaii's most famous restaurants.

In 1937, the restaurant was torn down and replaced by the present structure, which sports a dramatic Chinese architectural style and vibrant color scheme. "Wo Fat" means peace and prosperity. It is a fitting name for this establishment that seats 850, and is a favorite for parties and banquets. On the wall inside is an interesting collection of old photos of the early Chinese in Hawaii.

11. Hotel Street. The adventurous may enjoy a stroll down Hotel Street, but if you find porn shops and x-rated movie houses offensive, better bypass this area.

Hotel Street has long had a reputation for its bawdy side and has been a popular spot for visiting seamen and soldiers. Even in the late 1800s, it was estimated there were at least 300 prostitutes working this area. Don't be surprised if you see a few "ladies" even during the day.

Walking toward Waikiki on Hotel, turn left at Smith Street.

12. Ramsay Chinatown Gallery, 1128 Smith Street, open Monday through Friday, 12:00 - 5:00. Ramsay features retrospectives and solo and traveling shows of a different artist beginning the first Monday of each month. The gallery is housed in the Tan Sing building, which was built in 1923, and is on the National and State Register of Historic Places.

The gallery has been a favorite spot for film crews and photographers, and the *Magnum, P. I.,* crew has filmed here twice. The front wall sports Tom Selleck's autograph, along with a collection of autographs of other Honolulu celebrities.

In the courtyard you'll find a bronze sculpture by Chuck Watson entitled *Polynesia,* two Tropical Trolleys, fashioned after the muleldrawn trolleys used in Honolulu in the 1800s, and an antique printing press used for the first Chinese newspaper in Hawaii.

The Tan Sing building also houses the Arts Council, the Association of Hawaii Artists, Hawaii Craftsmen, and the Hawaii Heritage Center, which leads Chinatown tours on

Wednesdays and Fridays.

Walk back to Hotel Street to **13. Encore Saloon Building**, corner Hotel and Nuuanu. Built in 1886, this building is one of the few left in Chinatown that predates both fires. The building at one time was owned by J. P. Mendonca, a ranch luna (foreman). During the building's renovation in 1980, a small, hidden passage was discovered, which is believed to have been a hideout for shanghaied sailors.

Turn left on Nuuanu to **14. Lai Fong**, 1118 Nuuanu. This fascinating store is filled with oriental antiques, silk brocades from Hong Kong, ivory and jade jewelry, teakwood and rosewood furniture and numerous other treasures.

Lai Fong was a picture bride from Canton who came to Hawaii and quickly established herself as a skillful dress designer. She sold bolts of fabrics door to door and was soon able to open the store in the heart of Chinatown which is still operating nearly fifty years later. The store still specializes in tailor-made clothing, and women can order a custom-made silk *Cheong sam* (Chinese-style dress) for as little as $25.

The stone sidewalk in front of the store is made of granite blocks from China that were used aboard ships as ballast. These blocks are scattered throughout Chinatown and were also used in the construction of a few buildings that are still standing.

15. Pauahi Nuuanu Gallery, 1 North Pauahi, corner of Nuuanu. Open Monday through Friday, 10:30 a.m. to 4:00 p.m., Saturday, 9:00 a.m. to 1:00 p.m. Partners Lorna and Michael Dunne feature fine Hawaiian arts and crafts in native woods, traditional and contemporary trunks, *umeke* bowls and Niihau shell leis. Michael Dunne is the craftsman who creates the wooden bowls.

Turn right at Pauahi and go one block to Bethel. On the corner is **16. Hawaii Theatre**, a grand old dame from Hawaii's past. It was once the largest and best center for the performing arts in the state. The theatre was designed for both live performances and motion pictures, and can seat 1800 people. It opened officially on September 6, 1922, and was called the "Pride of the Pacific" by Governor Wallace Farrington Inside, the theatre is still a beauty and reflects the eclectic trends of the 20s and 30s with a mixture of Beaux Arts, classical columns, frescoes, murals, mosaics and art deco. It is on both the State and National Registers of Historic Places.

Go back to Nuuanu. Turn right and walk to **17. Pegge Hopper Gallery**, 1164 Nuuanu. Open Monday through Friday, 11:00 a.m. to 5:00 p.m., Saturday, 11:00 a.m. to 3:00 p.m. Ring the bell to be admitted. Hopper is renowned for her dramatic and colorful paintings of island women. Her work is in numerous private and public collections, including the State Foundation on Culture and Arts and the Contemporary Arts Center. Her gallery, situated in what used to be the Japanese quarter of Chinatown, features only her own work. She has original paintings, posters, serigraphs, lithographs, books and beach towels.

Continue up Nuuanu toward the mountains. Turn left at Beretania to **18. Sweetheart's Lei Shop**, 79A North Beretania. There are several lei shops along Maunakea and around the corner on Beretania. It's fascinating to stop and watch the lei-makers deftly and patiently stringing thousands of blossoms to create the lovely leis. Sweetheart's is run by the Lau family, who have been in business in Chinatown for over fifty-five years. For a special gift for someone, ask for a pikake or ilima lei.

Across Beretania you'll see **19. Sun Yat-sen Statue** at the end of River Street. Sun Yat-sen is considered the liberator of China and Father of the Chinese Republic.

Hawaii has been called the "cradle of the Chinese Republic" because of Sun Yat-sen's activities here. Sun came to Hawaii in 1878 at the age of twelve to join his older brother, Ah Mi, who supported him and sent him to Iolani School. Sun was an exceptional student, and learned English so rapidly that three years after he entered Iolani, speaking only Chinese, he was presented an award by King Kalakaua for his achievements in English.

It was also during his time at Iolani that Sun developed an interest in Christianity, and came to believe that much of the backwardness of China was due to the superstition and dread of evil spirits of his countrymen. He wanted to be baptized at Iolani, but his brother forbade it. After his graduation in 1882, Ah Mi sent him back to China in order to discourage his interest in Christianity and to fulfill his filial duty of marriage.

Sun completed his medical training and practiced medicine in Hong Kong until war broke out between China and Japan in 1894. He returned to Hawaii and formed the first chapter of the

Hsing Chung Hui (Revive China Party), which aimed to drive out the Manchu rulers and establish a Chinese Republic. The Hsing Chung Hui was one of the forerunners of the Tung Men Hui or Chinese Revolutionary Alliance, which launched the Chinese Revolution in 1911. The Iolani School graduate was made the first Provisional President of the new republic in 1912.

Sun Yat-sen's statue stands next to 20. **Chinatown Cultural Plaza**, 100 North Beretania, which consists mainly of small shops and restaurants. In the center of the Plaza is the Moongate Stage, where entertainment is held from time to time. Around the courtyard are several jewelry shops that offer good prices on pearl necklaces and jade jewelry.

Also inside the Plaza is the Dragon Gate Bookstore, which specializes in Chinese books, magazines, and cassette tapes. They also have a fair number of books in English covering topics such as Chinese herbal medicine, acupuncture, travel guides to China and Chinese history and politics.

On the second floor of the Plaza, above the Fortune Gate restaurant, is the Sun Yat-sen Hall and United Chinese Press. The walls of the hall are filled with photographs of Sun Yat-sen and his fellow revolutionaries. In the corner of the hall is the printing office of the United Chinese Press. Arrive before 10:30 a.m. and watch the printer hand-setting the Chinese type for this 35-year-old newspaper.

On the third floor above Hakubundo, the Chee Kong Tong Society has a lovely meeting hall with an elaborate Chinese decor and impressive shrine. The folks there say it's okay for visitors to take a quick peek.

Walk toward the mountains along the River Walk to Kukui Street. Across Nuuanu Stream is 21. **Izumo Taisha Shrine.** This is a Shinto temple enshrining Okuninushi No Mikoto, a *kami* (universal god), sometimes known as the dispenser of happiness and good marriage.

The shrine is over eighty years old, but the present structure was erected in 1923. There is no weekly Sunday service, but there are usually monthly services on the 10th of each month. A visit to the shrine is an ancient Japanese tradition to give thanks for the blessings of the past and to ask divine guidance and protection for the new year. Visitors are welcome, but please remove your shoes.

The Shinto
Bishop of the
Izumo Taisha
Temple

Cross Kukui Street and continue along the stream to Vineyard Boulevard. **22. Kuan Yin Temple** is the oldest and most frequented Chinese temple in Honolulu. It was first established in the 1880s and rebuilt several times. Here followers light candles and incense, say prayers and make offerings before one or more of the images.

On the center altar is Kuan Yin on a lotus blossom. On the right altar is Wei Tor, protector and guardian of the faith. On the left altar is Kuan Tai, protector of truth and justice.

Each object is symbolic; the lotus represents purity rising out of impurity, the pearl provides light, and the whisk brushes away evil. The altar offerings of fruits and flowers are products of what is sown and reaped.

Priests and priestesses in the temple offer advice through the use of joss sticks, which when shaken are believed to foretell the future on any subject.

Ancient legend tells that Kuan Yin was the youngest and most beautiful daughter of an ancient king of China. As she grew older she observed the many trials and tribulations that humanity had to endure. She vowed never to marry, but her father protested and threatened punishment. She became a nun, and the gods took pity on her and made her the Goddess of Mercy.

Visitors are welcome in the temple, but please show respect while others are worshipping, and take no flash pictures. A donation in the offering box helps sustain the temple.

The temple closes at 2:00 p.m. daily. Next door is Foster Botanical Gardens (See WALK 10).

For Guided Walks of Chinatown, see Walks 4 and 5 on page 93.

 ## WALK 8 - HISTORIC HONOLULU I

1 mile, one way
30 minutes

Begin this walk at the **Mission Houses,** corner of King and Kawaiahao Streets. If you want to tour the inside of the houses, they are open daily from 9:00 a.m. to 4:00 a.m.There is an admission charge.

The arrival of the missionaries in 1820 was one of the most important events in Hawaiian history. These mission houses, built by Congregational missionaries from New England, are the oldest structures in Honolulu. The two-story frame house was built in 1821 with materials shipped from Boston. The smallest building is the site of the first printing done in Hawaii. The missionaries translated the Christian scriptures into Hawaiian and produced primers, hymnals and bibles here. The largest of the three, Chamberlain House, was built in 1831.

The Mission Houses Museum presents a Living History program on Saturday, which begins every hour on the hour starting at 10:00 a.m. The last presentation begins at 2:30 p.m. This program recreates the people and events of 1831, complete with authentic costumes. It is included in the price of admission to the Museum.

Cross Kawaiahao Street and enter the Missionary's Cemetery behind **Kawaiahao Church.** In the Cemetery are buried several missionary families and their descendants. Hiram Bingham was the first to be buried here in 1823. Continue on around the Church and read all the historical markers relating the history of the area.

Kawaiahao was the first Christian church built in the islands, and is surely the most impressive and famous of the historical churches. It was the largest building in Hawaii until Iolani Palace was constructed in 1880-82.

The cornerstone was laid in 1837, and after five years of labor the church was dedicated on July 21, 1842. It was designed by

Reverend Hiram Bingham, leader of the missionaries, and over the years has been the site of many important events for Hawaiian royalty, such as christenings, marriages, and funerals. The building was built from nearly 14,000 coral blocks, and is on both the National and State Registers of Historic Buildings.

Visitors can tour the inside of the church daily between 9:00 a.m. and 3:00 p.m, and there are Sunday services in Hawaiian and English at 8:00 a.m. and 10:30 a.m.

In front of the Church is King Lunalilo's Tomb. He reigned for little more than a year and died on February 3, 1874, at the age of forty-two. He asked to be buried at Kawaiahao among the people rather than at the Royal Mausoleum with kings and chiefs.

Cross King Street at Punchbowl, and visit **Honolulu Hale**, or City Hall. This Spanish-style building, completed in 1929, houses the office of the Mayor of Honolulu, the City Council and other municipal government agencies.

In front of the building is a Japanese garden displaying a 2,000-lb. stone lantern that was presented to the City in 1957 by the Mayor of Yokohama, and a stone pagoda presented in 1968

Kawaiahao Church (Photo courtesy of Hawaii Visitors Bureau)

by the City of Hiroshima.

During normal working hours, you can tour the inside. The beautiful courtyard, stairway and open ceiling were modeled after a 13th century palace in Florence, Italy. Notice the handmade chandeliers and the frescoes on the ceiling. There is a gallery in the first floor, right-hand corner of the building, which has frequent art exhibits.

Backtrack across King Street and continue walking away from Diamond Head until you see the gold and black statue of **King Kamehameha** on the left.

In 1878, the Legislature appropriated $10,000 for a "heroic statue in bronze" of King Kamehameha the Great. T. R. Gould, a Boston artist, created the statue in 1879 and had it cast in Paris. On its way to the Islands, the ship carrying the statue sank near the Falkland Islands. The work was insured, and a duplicate was made. In the meantime, the original was salvaged and set up in Hawaii on the Big Island, near Kamehameha's birthplace. There is another copy of this statue in Statuary Hall in Washington, D.C.

Behind the statue is **Ali'iolani Hale**, or the Judiciary Building, which was designed in 1869 as a residence for Kamehameha V. He had little interest in having a palace for a home, and decided it should be used for administrative offices instead.

Directly across King Street is **Iolani Palace**. If you'd like to tour the inside, there are tours between 9:00 a.m. and 2:15 p.m. Wednesday through Saturday. There is an admission charge.

In December of 1879, the cornerstone of the Palace was laid by King Kalakaua, who took up residence in 1882. Until 1893, the palace was the official home for the monarchy until Queen Lili'uokalani was deposed by a group of American businessmen who abolished the monarchy and took over the government.

Restoration of the Palace was begun in 1970 by the Parks Division of the Department of Land and Natural Resources and the Friends of Iolani Palace.

Next door to the palace is Iolani Barracks, which formerly housed the Royal Household Guards. The Barracks were built in 1870 near the site of the State Capitol and were moved in 1965 to the present location.

On the front lawn of the palace is the Coronation Pavilion of King Kalakaua, which is now referred to as the bandstand. The

Iolani Palace (Photo courtesy of Hawaii Visitors Bureau)

Royal Hawaiian Band presents concerts here at noon on Fridays.

Across the lawn, toward the library, you'll notice the first royal mausoleum, which was built in 1825 to house the remains of King Kamehameha II and Queen Kamamalu. In 1865, when the new mausoleum was built in Nuuanu Valley, the sacred bones of the royal dead were moved to their new home.

Walk around behind the palace, and you'll notice two huge banyan trees that are said to have been planted by Queen Kapiolani in 1882.

The unusual-looking building behind the Palace is the **State Capitol**. The design of this building is unlike any other capitol in the country. All of the elements of the design of the building are symbolic of Hawaii's unique characteristics. The 60-foot columns surrounding the building are meant to suggest the royal palms that used to line the entrance to many of Hawaii's fine old homes. The four reflecting pools symbolize the sea that surrounds the islands. The cone-shaped Legislative Chambers symbolize the volcanoes that created the islands.

There are also many fine works of art around the Capitol, including, in the center of the courtyard, a mosaic by Tadashi Sato, which is made of 600,000 pieces of mosaic tile from Italy.

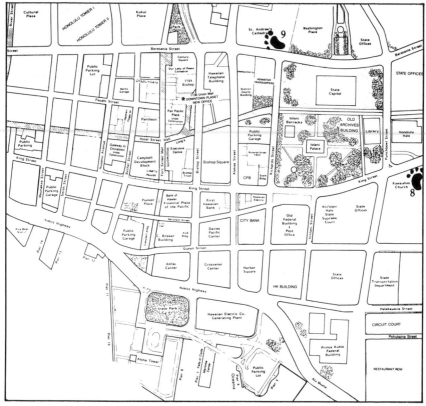

Downtown Honolulu

On the Beretania Street side of the Capitol is a statue of Father Damien, created by the Venezuelan sculptress Marisol. This statue is a duplicate of an original placed in Statuary Hall in the U.S. Capitol in Washington, D.C.

Visitors can arrange a tour of the building in the Sergeant-at-Arms office, in room 036. The tour lasts about an hour and includes a 30-minute presentation describing the symbolism of the building, an overview of Hawaii's politics, and a visit to the Governor's and Lt. Governor's offices. Call 548-7851 for reservations.

Cross Beretania Street and you'll see double rows of royal palms and a memorial designed by Bumpei Akaji. The eternal flame was lighted in October 1974 as a memorial to the men and women of Hawaii who served in the Armed Forces of the U.S.

Continue walking along Beretania away from Diamond

Head, and the next building you'll come to is **Washington Place**. This beautiful estate has been the home of Hawaii's Governors since 1922. It was built in 1846 as the home of John Dominis, a merchant from Boston. Dominis' son, John Owen Dominis, married High Chiefess Lydia Kamakaleha Kapalakea, who became Queen Lili'uokalani in 1891. She was deposed from the throne in 1893 and for eight months she was imprisoned in Iolani Palace. Afterwards she returned to Washington Place, where she lived until her death on November 11, 1917, at the age of seventy.

The house has been restored several times and contains many historic works of art. The inside can be visited only by invitation of the Governor's family.

If you want to return to King Street, turn left and walk two blocks, or if you want to continue, see WALK 9.

For a Guided Walk beginning at the Mission Houses, see Walk 6 on page 93.

 WALK 9 - HISTORIC HONOLULU II   1 mile, one way
1/2-1 hour

This walk begins next door to Washington Place, where WALK 8 ends. The impressive building on the corner of Beretania and Alakea is **Saint Andrew's Cathedral**.

To combat the influence of America's missionaries in Hawaii, Kamehameha IV sought assistance from Britain and the Anglican faith. In 1862, Right Reverend Thomas Staley, the first Anglican Bishop of Honolulu, and his family sailed from London for Hawaii. Kamehameha IV did not live to see the establishment of the first Anglican church, but Kamehameha V, his brother, laid the cornerstone of St. Andrew's in 1867 and declared it a memorial to his predecessor.

Blocks of sandstone were shipped from England, but they were not set in place for more than 15 years. The entire cathedral took 91 years to complete.

The front is dominated by a fountain and statue of St. Andrew, Patron Saint of the Cathedral. The figure of Andrew was created by sculptor Ivan Mestrovic, and the fish by Robert Laurent. The magnificent Great West Window is one of the largest stained glass windows ever constructed in the U.S. It was designed by John Wallis in 1956, and is made of handblown glass from France, Germany, Belgium, England and the U.S. The window's symbolism tells the history of the Christian Church. The fountain and the stained glass window were completed in 1958.

Cross Beretania and walk two blocks farther to the end of the Fort Street Mall, which ends at Beretania. Here you'll see the first Catholic church built in the islands, the **Cathedral of Our Lady of Peace.**

The first group of Catholic missionaries arrived in Hawaii in 1827, but met much opposition from the Protestant missionaries and ruling chiefs. The Catholics were banished from the islands in 1837, but returned in 1839 when Kamehameha III granted freedom of worship to his people. In 1843, the Catholic missionaries began building this cathedral, and it was here that Joseph de Veuster, a young Belgian, was ordained a priest in 1864. He chose the name of Damien, and became a hero to the Hawaiian people for his lifelong work with leprosy patients who were banished to the Island of Molokai.

Walk up the Fort Street Mall toward the ocean. Fort Street derived its name from a fort that was built near the Harbor in 1816. The fort was destroyed in 1857.

After crossing Merchant Street, you'll find two structures that are on the National Register of Historic Places. Facing the mall at 827 Fort Street is the **C. Brewer** building, completed in 1930. This Mediterranean-style building has housed the corporate offices for C. Brewer & Co. for almost sixty years. The company's history dates back to 1826, when James Hunnewell arrived in Honolulu with 40 barrels of assorted "yankee goods" for sale.

Around the corner, facing Bishop Street, is the **Alexander & Baldwin** building, completed in 1929. This outstanding structure includes Chinese, Mediterranean, Italian, Buddhist, Tibetan, Japanese and Hawaiian elements in its design. Notice the beautiful tile murals of Hawaiian fish near the main entrance, and the decorative tile work on the ceiling. If you're passing by during business hours, you can step inside and ask the receptionist for a brochure about the building. Alexander & Baldwin is one of Hawaii's "Big Five" companies, which have dominated the local corporate scene for many years. A & B was formed as a partnership in 1870 and incorporated in 1900.

Backtrack to the Fort Street Mall, and continue on across Queen Street to **Walker Park** behind the Amfac buildings. Read the historical markers around the lawn, and notice the cannon that came from the Fort that used to be located near here. Facing the building, you'll see an entrance on the right that says **Amfac Plaza**, where a new art exhibit is presented each month. It's usually open during business hours, and there is no admission charge.

Continue on across Nimitz at the crosswalk to Irwin Park, a little green oasis that fronts the Honolulu Harbor and the **Aloha Tower**. Go up the escalator and continue walking straight to the end of the walkway. Enter the door on the right and follow the signs up to the Aloha Tower Observation Deck.

The Aloha Tower was built in 1921 and is Hawaii's version of the Statue of Liberty. It greets ships arriving in Honolulu Harbor and houses the harbor traffic controller's station. An observation deck on the tenth floor offers a spectacular view of the harbor, downtown Honolulu and the coast. The observation deck is open from 8:00 a.m. to 9:00 p.m. daily, and there is no admission charge.

Honolulu Harbor's history began around 1792, when British Captain William Brown discovered an inlet along Oahu's southern coast called Kou. It was the only accessible harbor in the islands, and before long became known as Honolulu, Hawaiian for "sheltered harbor."

Increasing numbers of foreign ships sailed into the harbor, and it soon became the most important place in Hawaii. King Kamehameha I moved his home here in 1803, about where Pier 12 is today. On the point of land where Aloha Tower stands was a heiau, or temple, dedicated to Lono.

On the Diamond Head side of the Observation Deck, you can see the *Falls of Clyde* and the new **Maritime Center**, your next stop. Backtrack down to the street level, and walk along next to the pier until you get to the *Falls of Clyde*. If you want to tour the ship, there is an admission charge that includes the Maritime Center also. They are open daily from 9:00 a.m. to 5:00 p.m.

The *Falls of Clyde* is the sole surviving four-masted sailing vessel in the world. She was built in 1878 in Glasgow, Scotland, and from 1879 to 1899 voyaged to ports around the world carrying general cargo. In 1898, she was purchased by William

Aloha Tower
(Photo courtesy
of Hawaii Visi-
tors Bureau)

Matson as the first of the Matson Line vessels. She arrived in
Honolulu on January 20, 1899.

In 1907, she was sold to the Associated Oil Company, and
was converted to a sailing oil tanker. In 1963, the people of
Hawaii raised the funds to buy her and bring her back to
Honolulu in order to save her from being destroyed.

Next to the ship is the new $6 million Kalakaua Boathouse,
which houses the Maritime Museum, displaying exhibits which
span the 2,000-year history of Hawaii's seafaring heritage.
Visitors can discover how the Polynesians sailed by the stars in
double-hulled canoes, relive the days of the whalers, or see
exciting video displays of surfers and windsurfers.

On the pier behind the museum, overlooking the Harbor, is
Coasters, a two-story, open-air restaurant that is a pleasant
place to take a rest and have lunch.

Foster Gardens banyan

WALK 10 - FOSTER BOTANICAL GARDENS *(180 N. Vineyard Blvd.)*

5.5 acres
45 minutes

The gardens are open daily from 9:00 a.m. to 4:00 p.m., and there is a $1.00 admission charge. At the front desk pick up the"Self-guided Tour" booklet, which has a map and descriptions of several of the items in the gardens. Be sure to look for the Bo tree, Chinese Banyan, Bromeliad Garden, Orchid Garden, Sausage Tree, Cannonball tree and the Daibutsu statue.

These gardens trace their beginning to 1855, when Queen Kalama sold this property to William Hillebrand, a young German doctor. The magnificent trees towering in the center of the gardens were planted by him.

He returned to Germany in 1867 and sold the property to Captain and Mrs. Thomas Foster. They continued to develop the garden until 1930, when they bequeathed the 5.5-acre site to the City of Honolulu as a public tropical botanical garden. Dr. Harold Lyon was named the first director of the garden, and over a period of 27 years he introduced 10,000 new kinds of trees and plants to Hawaii. The Foster Gardens orchid collection was started with his own plants.

Today the gardens have expanded to 20 acres, and are now part of Honolulu Botanical Gardens, which together with the Wahiawa Botanical Garden, Ho'omaluhia and Koko Crater Botanical Garden encompass 650 acres.

For a Guided Walk of Foster Gardens, see Walk 7 on p. 93.

 WALK 11 - PUNCHBOWL   1.5 miles
(NATIONAL MEMORIAL   30-45 minutes
CEMETERY OF THE PACIFIC)
(2177 Puowaina Drive)

Punchbowl crater was called *Puowaina* (hill of sacrifice) by the ancient Hawaiians because human sacrifices were made here. Today, the crater contains a 68-acre cemetery sometimes called the "Arlington of the Pacific." Construction of the cemetery began in 1948, and today it is the resting place for more than 20,000 military personnel. It is one of the state's top visitor attractions.

There are two drives that circle the inside of the crater. Inner Drive is about 1/2-mile around, and Outer Drive is about 1 mile. The information office has a free map of the inside of the crater.

In the center of the cemetery you'll notice a War Memorial, with marble tablets recording the names of 28,745 men whose bodies were never recovered in World War II, Korea and Vietnam. The Memorial also contains murals illustrating the events of World War II.

If you walk up the center drive toward the Memorial, you'll see the grave of Astronaut Ellison Onizuka on the left. You can walk around the roadway and up to an overlook on the rim of the crater, which provides a spectacular panoramic view of Honolulu.

The gates are open from 8:00 a.m. to 5:30 p.m. daily.

Punchbowl Cemetery (Photo courtesy of Hawaii Visitors Bureau)

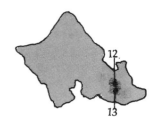

Manoa Valley

 WALK 12- LYON ARBORETUM

124 acres
30-45 minutes

Near the top of Manoa Road, above Paradise Park, is a lush 124-acre arboretum that is owned by the University of Hawaii. At the front desk, pick up a "self-guided tour" brochure, which has a map of the arboretum. Visiting hours are from 9:00 a.m. to 3:00 p.m. daily. The Lyon Arboretum Association also offers classes and hikes to other areas.

Hawaiians used to call this area *Haukulu* (the land of the dripping dew), but by 1918 grazing cattle had denuded it. The Hawaii Sugar Planters' Association established a program to restore the area, and appointed Dr. Harold Lyon, who gathered

41

seeds and plants from all over the world. In 1953 the arboretum was presented to the University of Hawaii.

Today, the arboretum contains over 900 genera and 4,000 species and varieties of trees and shrubs. There are also specialized collections, including an Ethnobotanical Garden that includes dozens of species that were important to native Hawaiians. The Harold Lyon Arboretum Memorial Garden contains a collection of trees, shrubs, ferns and flowers cross-referenced to a chart that helps identify each.

For a Guided Walk of Lyon Arboretum, see Walk 8, page 93.

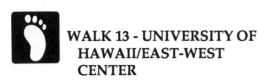

WALK 13 - UNIVERSITY OF HAWAII/EAST-WEST CENTER

.75 miles, one way
30-45 minutes

Parking is limited at the University during school sessions, so it's best to ride the bus or visit on the weekend. The University campus, covering 320 acres in Manoa Valley, offers many points of interest, including fascinating architecture, over 500 varieties of tropical flora and over 20 major works of art which adorn the campus.

The University was founded in 1907 as the College of Agriculture and Mechanic Arts of the Territory of Hawaii. It became the University of Hawaii in 1920 and now has nine campuses and a student body of over 50,000.

Begin the walk at **Bachman Hall**, which houses the administrative offices of the University President and Board of Regents. The building, which was built in 1949, also contains two murals by Jean Charlot. The first floor mural is of Captain James Cook's arrival in Hawaii in 1778. It depicts "The Relationship of Man and Nature in Old Hawaii." A mural on the second floor is of parents greeting graduates with leis. Both murals were completed in the '50s.

Walk out on the lawn in front of Bachman. On the right, toward Sinclair Library, you'll see a cannonball tree, one of the many interesting trees around the campus. The hard, brown fruits make it obvious how the tree got its name. This member of the Brazil nut family also produces unusual, waxy-looking flowers, which sit atop tangles of stems around the trunk.

As you face the corner of University Avenue and Dole Street, you'll see **Founder's Gate**, which was built in 1933, symbolizing the merging of two separate campuses: the University and the Territorial Normal School, the predecessor to the College of Education. The Hawaiian phrases on the archways are: *Maluna a'e o no lahui opau ke ola ke kanaka* (above all nations is humanity) and *Hoolaaia no na poe apau no na makahiki lehulehu i hooka wowa i ka hoonaauao akea ma Hawaii nei* (dedicated to all those who through the many years fostered the cause of public education in Hawaii).

Behind Bachman is **Andrews Outdoor Theatre**, built in 1935. This outdoor theatre has over 5,000 seats made of stone from different campus sites. It has been the site of numerous concerts, commencement exercises and other campus activities.

Walk around to the front of **Sinclair Library**, where you'll find an assortment of interesting trees, including a sandbox tree, which has heart-shaped leaves and pumpkin-shaped fruits. The fruits were once used as containers for sand for blotting letters. You'll probably find the split seed cases along the walkway beneath the tree. These are often used in making jewelry.

Sinclair Library is one of two major libraries on the campus that house more than two million volumes and special Hawaiian, Pacific and Asian collections.

Next to the library is **Hemenway Hall**, built in 1938. This building was the center for student activities for many years. It was also the first building on campus used for non-academic purposes. Now it's an extension of the larger Campus Center next door. Hemenway houses a crafts center offering a variety of non-credit classes, and a theater.

Walking along Campus Road toward the Campus Center, you'll notice one of the many sculptures gracing the campus. *Hina 0 Na Lani* (Mother of the Universe), a granite sculpture at the entryway to the Campus Center, was produced in 1975 by Gregory Clurman.

In 1967 Hawaii became the first state in the nation to adopt an Art in State Buildings Law that requires setting aside 1% of construction appropriations for new state buildings to be used for art work. More than twenty major works around the campus were created by both local and other artists as part of this program.

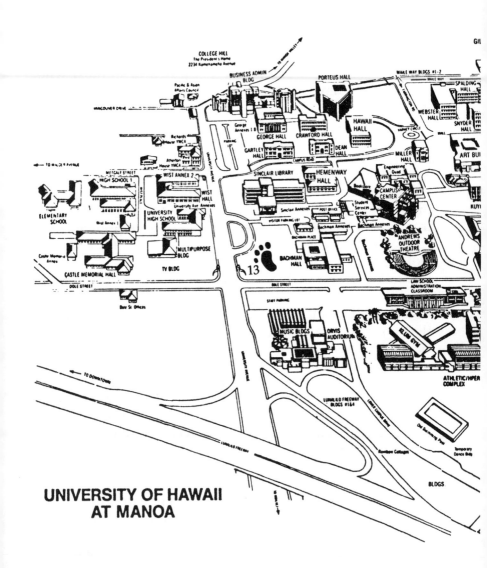

UNIVERSITY OF HAWAII
AT MANOA

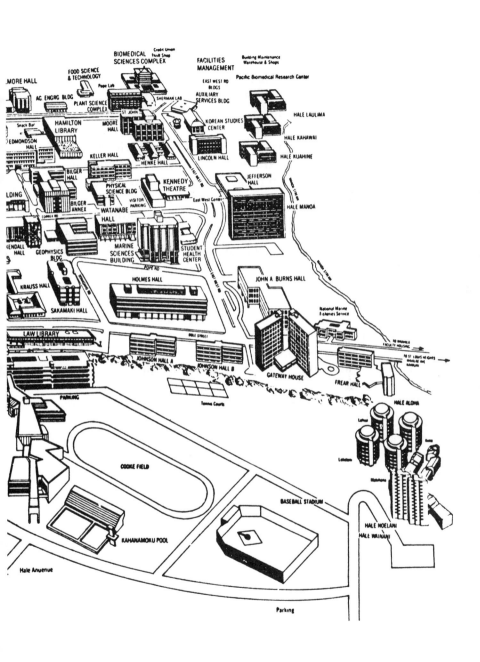

Map courtesy of the University of Hawaii

The **Campus Center** houses a bookstore, a cafeteria, a small art exhibit area, and a beautiful mural depicting scenes of local culture.

Proceeding along Campus Road past the Campus Center, you'll see a breadfruit tree. The breadfruit ('ulu) is still a staple in the diets of many Pacific islanders.

Next you'll encounter the sausage tree, a native of West Africa. The sausage-looking fruits are non-edible, but have been used as external medicine.

Behind the sausage tree is an African tulip tree with clusters of bright orange tulip-shaped flowers. In Ghana, it is known as *baton de Sorcier* because the blossoms are said to be used by witch doctors for black magic.

To your left is **Varney Circle**, with a fountain built in 1934. The design depicts a Hawaiian god, bordered by palm fronds.

Hawaii Hall, facing the circle, was built in 1912, and was the first permanent building of the University. It was originally called the Main Building, and was renamed Hawaii Hall in 1922.

Walk around to the front of Hawaii Hall and you'll be in an area called the **Quadrangle**, which consists of Gartley Hall (1922), George Hall (1925), Dean Hall (1929) and Crawford Hall (1938). These four buildings, along with Hawaii Hall, formed the core of the Manoa campus for many years.

The royal palms in front of George Hall were planted by the graduating class of 1926.

Continue on around Hawaii Hall. Looking toward Porteus Hall, you'll notice a Bo tree, the sacred tree of Buddhism. It was under a similar tree that Prince Gautama received his enlightenment. This tree was planted by the first graduating class of the Manoa campus in 1912.

Walk back to Varney Circle and visit the **Art Building,** on the right just past the Circle. On the ewa side of the building you'll see an interesting tree with the name of "dead rat" tree. It received its name because its fuzzy fruits hanging from long stems look like dead rats. This tropical tree is a native of Africa.

Near the entrance of the Art Building, on the mall, is a sculpture named *The Fourth Sign* (the zodiacal sign of Cancer). This ten-ton, steel, crab-like sculpture was donated by the artist Tony Smith in 1976. Next to the sculpture are three tamarind trees, natives of Asia and Tropical Africa. The tree's reddish-brown pods contain a sweet-sour pulp which is used in drinks, curries, chutneys and medicine, and is rich in B vitamins.

Explore the Art Building's bamboo-lined garden courtyard and two art galleries.

On the mall, at the corner of the Art Building and Bilger Hall is a Hutu tree. This distinctive tree has large woody fruits and white flowers that resemble shaving brushes. It grows throughout the Pacific, and has seeds that were used by Polynesians to create a mixture that would stupefy fish when it was thrown into the water.

Inside **Bilger Hall** you'll find *Water*, a mural by Honolulu artist David Asherman, depicting the Hawaiian god Kane bringing forth water to create Manoa Stream.

On the exterior wall of the **Physical Science Building,** facing Bilger Annex, is a fun mural, *The Great Manoa Crack Seed Caper*, which was painted by an art class in 1981.

The large structure across the mall is **Hamilton Library.** Near the main entrance is a bronze, steel and granite sculpture by Harold Tovish, entitled *Epitaph*. Inside the library entrance area is a batik by artist Yvonne Cheng entitled *Nana I Ke Kumu* (Look to the Source).

Continuing down the mall to **Henke Hall**, enter the courtyard and you'll find guava and Surinam cherry trees. Guava was brought to Hawaii early in the nineteenth century from tropical America, and today is one of the most common wild fruit trees in Hawaii.

The Surinam cherry is a Brazilian tree that produces a small, red, pumpkin-shaped fruit that is used in drinks, jellies and pies.

At the end of the mall, turn left on East-West Road. The elaborate building on the right is the **Korean Studies Center,** which was built in 1979 and patterned after Kyongbok Palace in Seoul.

Turn around and walk along East-West Road toward Dole Street. On the left you'll come to the **Thai Pavilion**, between Jefferson and Lincoln Halls. This fascinating structure was given to the University by King Bhumbibol Adulyadej and Queen Sirikit of Thailand in 1965. Teak pavilions such as this are common throughout Thailand, and are used as places of contemplation.The Pavilion is surrounded by several Chinese banyans, also called laurel fig in other parts of the world.

Near the flagpole of **Jefferson Hall** are several Singapore plumerias, natives of the West Indies, which were introduced into Hawaii by Dr. Harold Lyon in 1931.

Next on the left is Jefferson Hall, one of the most attractive buildings on the campus. Jefferson Hall was completed in 1963 and contains an information center, a reading area, a large lanai that overlooks a Japanese garden and carp stream, international conference rooms and several murals by Jean Charlot, Affandi, and David Parker. It is also the heart of the **East-West Center**, a federally-funded educational institution designed to promote mutual understanding among the peoples of Asia, the Pacific and the U.S. The Center was established in 1960 by the U.S. Congress, and is located on 21 acres of University land .

Behind Jefferson Hall is **Jakuan** (Cottage of Tranquility), an authentic teahouse given to the University in 1972 by the Urasenke School of the Tea Ceremony. Students of *chado* (the way of tea) learn the art of communicating delight in beauty, hospitality, communion and peace in the teahouse.

The lovely **Japanese garden** is one of the highlights of the campus. *"Seien"* (peaceful garden) was designed by Kenzo Ogata of Tokyo, and was a gift of Japanese businessmen. The central focus of the garden is a stream built in the shape of the Chinese character *kokorol* (heart, spirit). The stream is filled with carp provided by the Hawaii Goldfish and Carp Association. Among the plants in the garden are a willow from the Imperial Palace grounds in Tokyo and a pink shower tree planted in 1964 by Crown Prince Akihito and Princess Michiko of Japan.

This is the end of WALK 13. Feel free to explore the rest of the campus, visit the libraries, or have lunch at the Campus Center Cafeteria (closed on weekends).

For Guided Walks of the University and East-West Center, see Walks 9 and 10 on pages 93 and 94.

Hawaii Kai

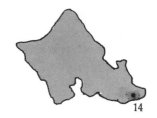

WALK 14 - KOKO CRATER   1 mile
BOTANICAL GARDEN   45 minutes
(Inside Koko Crater, off Kealahou Street)

Park in the small parking area and follow the path which starts out in a plumeria grove.

The 200-acres inside the volcanic cinder cone are part of the Honolulu Botanical Gardens and contain an interesting collection of cacti and succulents. Unfortunately, the plants are not labeled, but you may recognize a few.

The trail makes a loop through the base of Koko Crater, which is shared by the Koko Crater Stables. You may catch sight of a few horses and riders. The trail is easy walking, takes about 45 minutes, and brings you back where you started.

Foster Gardens sometimes leads guided walks through the crater with commentary by local botanists. (See Guided Walk 11, page 94.)

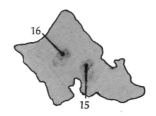

Moanalua/ Wahiawa

WALK 15 - MOANALUA GARDENS   1 mile
(Off H-l at Pu'uloa)   30-40 minutes

This garden is small, but picturesque and interesting.

It is a pleasant place to take the whole family, with plenty of room for kids to roam, but doesn't require too much walking.

Kids will be intrigued with the koi pond and ducks near the

summer cottage, which belonged to King Kamehameha V, and the Chinese Hall.

The Gardens also contain beautiful 100-year-old monkeypod trees and a variety of other fauna.

The Moanalua Gardens Foundation sponsors a tour of the Gardens (see Guided Walk 12, page 95) and also leads a 5-mile walk into the valley behind the Gardens. Call 839-5334 for more information.

The Gardens are also the site of the annual Prince Lot Hula Festival on the third Saturday of July. This day-long festival of ancient and modern hula also features exhibitions and demonstrations of Hawaiian arts, crafts and games.

 WALK 16 - WAHIAWA BOTANICAL   27 acres
GARDEN   30 minutes
(1396 California Avenue in Wahiawa)

Wahiawa Botanical Garden is part of the Honolulu BotanicalGardens, and covers a 27-acre wooded gulch.

The Gardens are open daily from 9:00 a.m. to 4:00 p.m., and admission is free. Stop at the front desk and pick up a brochure, which includes a map and description of some of the plants.

The trail winds around the garden, down through the gulch. Several of the most interesting specimens are labeled, such as the Mindanao Gum, the 'ie'ie, and the loulu. The Garden contains many exotics, and a new section is being developed which features native Hawaiian plants.

In the 1920s, the garden was used by the Hawaii Sugar Planters' Association for forestry experiments and as a nursery. It was turned over to the City and County of Honolulu in 1950 for the purpose of building a botanical garden.

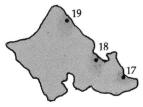

Windward Oahu
Kailua • Kaneohe • Laie

 WALK 17 - KAILUA BEACH   3 miles, round trip
(Off Kawialoa Rd. in Kailua)   45 minutes -1 hour

This is one of Oahu's most scenic places for taking a long beach stroll. The beach is about 1.5 miles long, and is especially lovely during the early morning or late afternoon hours when it's not too hot.

You can begin the walk at the Kailua Beach Park, a 30-acre park at the eastern end of Kailua Bay. This is an excellent swimming area and is also a fun spot to watch the sailors and windsurfers.

Around Alala Point to the right of the Beach Park is Lanikai, an upscale residential area. When the tide is down you can continue walking around the point and along Lanakai Beach. In 1925, Charles Frazier developed the Lanikai subdivision and also erected the monument resembling a lighthouse that stands at Alala Point.

The small islands offshore are State Bird Sanctuaries, and are popular spots with boaters. Visitors are supposed to obtain a permit from the State Division of Fish and Game.

 WALK 18 - HO'OMALUHIA   400 acres
BOTANICAL GARDEN   1-2 hours
(End of Luluku Road in Kaneohe)

This 400-acre botanical garden and nature conservancy is planted with trees and shrubs from different regions of the world. Ho'omaluhia is more like a forest preserve than a botanical garden. It is full of trees, bushes, vines, flowers, and fruits. Special emphasis has been placed on preserving and increasing the plants native and unique to Hawaii.

The visitor center has a brochure that contains a map of the park trails. There are also camping areas and educational programs. The gates are open from 9:00 a.m. to 3:00 p.m. daily.

Ho'omaluhia was designed and built by the U.S. Army Corps of Engineers to provide flood protection for Kaneohe. The area contains a 32-acre lake, hiking and horse trails, a community center, exhibition hall and classrooms.

For Guided Walks of Ho'omaluhia, see Walks 13, 14, 15, and 16 on page 94.

 WALK 19 - MALAEKAHANA　　2 miles, round trip
BEACH　　30-45 minutes
(On Kamehameha Hwy. in Laie)

This long stretch of beach offers one of the more lengthy and sparsely populated beach walks on the island.

Enter the Malaekahana Beach Park and park in the lot. There are restroom, picnic and camping facilities, and it's a pleasant place to spend the day.

Walk through the park toward the ocean and start the walk anywhere along the beach. You can walk over a mile in either direction.

Offshore from the park is Moku'auia or Goat Island. The more adventurous may enjoy walking across the narrow channel to the island, which is an official State Bird Refuge. It's best to cross at low tide on a calm day, and you should wear something to protect your feet from the coral. The water crossing the channel is about waist deep for an adult.

The island became known as Goat Island during the 1800s when residents of Laie attempted to raise goats, but later moved them to the island after discovering how destructive they were.

Island of Hawaii

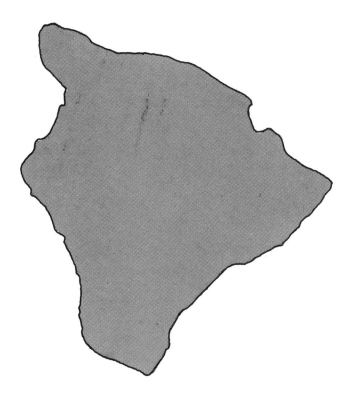

Hilo

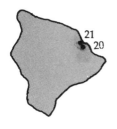

21
20

 WALK 20 - HISTORIC HILO   1 mile, one way
1 hour

This walk will take about one hour, and the fourteen stops along the way will provide you with information about the history of Hilo, which began with the arrival of the Polynesians in 1100 A.D. They inhabited the shores of Hilo Bay, farmed their crops, fished and traded their goods with each other along the Wailuku River. Changes came to this lifestyle upon the arrival of missionaries, who brought with them new ideas, education and Christianity.

Hilo became a stopping place for explorers curious about the active volcanoes, whaling ships and traders. By the 1900s, a number of wharves had been constructed, the breakwater was begun and the new railroad connected Hilo with other parts of the island. Hilo became the center of commerce. Two destructive tsunamis (tidal waves), in 1946 and 1960, caused a shift in the location of Hilo's government and commercial life.

Begin the walk at **1. Kalakaua Park** on the corners of Kalakaua and Kinoole Streets. This park is named after King Kalakaua, and there is a bronze statue of Hawaii's last king in the center of the park. The taro leaf at his left side symbolizes the Hawaiian people's bond with the land. The *ipu* on his right signifies the culture, chants and hula which he is credited with reviving.

Hilo became a favorite visiting place of the King, who designed the first county complex at this site in the late 19th century. At one time a courthouse and police station were part of this complex. The park contains a sundial bearing the inscription, "This sundial was erected in the Fourth Year of the reign of King Kalakaua, A.D. 1877, Hilo, Hawaii." It is thought that some of the trees in the park were planted during Kalakaua's time, making them over one hundred years old.

While in the park, notice the War Memorial adjacent to the

reflecting pool. Also look toward the mountains to the Hilo Hotel. Niolopa, the home of King Kalakaua and other Hawaiian royalty, was once located here.

Cross Kalakaua Street and stop on the sidewalk in front of the **2. Old Police Station**, which was vacated by the Hilo County Police Department in 1979. Today it is the home of the East Hawaii Cultural Center, an organization dedicated to culture and the arts in the East Hawaii area. Designed by Deputy Engineer Frank Arakawa, it was completed in 1932. The building resembles a Hawaiian *hale* (house) of the 1800s. It has been placed on the National Register of Historic Buildings and Places. There is no admission charge, and it is open Monday through Saturday from 9:00 a.m. to 4:00 p.m.

Walk downhill on Kalakaua Street and stop at the **3. Hawaiian Telephone Company Building**, right next to the Old Police Station. C. W. Dickey is credited with developing Hawaiian Regional Architecture in the early 20th century. Dickey was influenced by buildings of southern European countries such as Spain and Italy, the California Mission style and the Hawaiian hale. Note the high-hipped green tile roof and the brightly colored terra cotta tiles set in the building. The ohia lehua trees planted in front of the Hawaiian Telephone Building have yellow rather than the more common red flowers.

Continue down Kalakaua Street until you reach Keawe Street. Turn right and walk to Haili Street. Cross Haili Street and turn right. Walk up the hill to the **4. Central Christian Church**. Haili Street at one time was called Church Street because there were five churches along its route. Today three remain, one of which is the Central Christian Church. It was built for the Portuguese-speaking community in the early 1900s. The two buildings on the property look much the way they did when they were built. The smaller building was formerly the parsonage and has now been converted to a retail space.

Cross Kilauea Avenue and turn left. Walk down Kilauea Avenue to the **5. Taishoji Soto Mission**, established in 1913 by the Zen Buddhists. In earlier times there were 800 members. Today 300 members continue to worship at this mission.

Continue along Kilauea avenue until you get to Furneaux Lane. Turn left onto the lane and walk toward the ocean. This

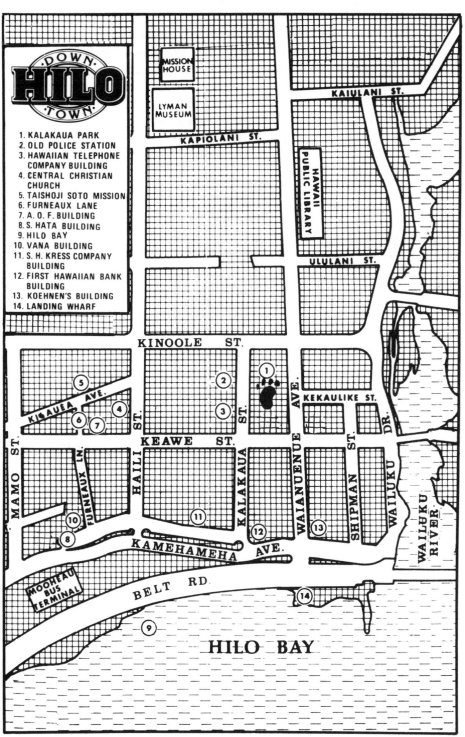

DOWN HILO TOWN

1. KALAKAUA PARK
2. OLD POLICE STATION
3. HAWAIIAN TELEPHONE COMPANY BUILDING
4. CENTRAL CHRISTIAN CHURCH
5. TAISHOJI SOTO MISSION
6. FURNEAUX LANE
7. A. O. F. BUILDING
8. S. HATA BUILDING
9. HILO BAY
10. VANA BUILDING
11. S. H. KRESS COMPANY BUILDING
12. FIRST HAWAIIAN BANK BUILDING
13. KOEHNEN'S BUILDING
14. LANDING WHARF

MISSION HOUSE

LYMAN MUSEUM

KAIULANI ST.

KAPIOLANI ST.

HAWAII PUBLIC LIBRARY

ULULANI ST.

KINOOLE ST.

KEKAULIKE ST.

KISAUEA AVE.

KEAWE ST.

MAMO ST.

HAILI ST.

FURNEAUX LN.

KALAKAUA ST.

WAIANUENUE AVE.

SHIPMAN ST.

WAILUKU DR.

WAILUKU RIVER

KAMEHAMEHA AVE.

MOOHEAU BUS TERMINAL

BELT RD.

HILO BAY

Reprinted from "Discover Downtown Hilo," with permission of the Hilo Downtown Improvement Association

57

narrow lane is named after Charles Furneaux, a prominent Hilo citizen during the turn of the century. He was an artist and amateur photographer who liked to record romantic scenes of life in Hilo.

Continue walking down Furneaux Lane and cross Keawe Street. Stop and look back at the **7. A.O.F. Building**, which is still used by the Ancient Order of Foresters. King Kalakaua was a member of this fraternal order. The building was constructed in 1925 in Renaissance revival style with arched entryways, balconies and columns used for decorative purposes.

Walk along Furneaux Lane until you reach Kamehameha Avenue. Cross the parking area. You should be standing on a planted strip bordering the parking lot. Turn to your right and walk until you are standing across from **8. S. Hata Building**. This is another example of Renaissance revival architecture. Notice the arched windows and decorative additions to the front of the building. Built by the Hata family in 1912, it was confiscated by the U. S. Government during World War II as property belonging to aliens. A daughter of the original owner bought the building back from the government for $100,000 when the war was over. Today the Hata family dry goods business is still carried on in this building.

Turn so that you are looking at **9. Hilo Bay**, with its black sand beach. Tsunamis in 1946 and 1960 traveled across the bay and hit the town, causing much destruction to commercial buildings located on both sides of Kamehameha Avenue. Today some of the original buildings remain on the side of the avenue farthest from the ocean. The area now planted with coconut palms and grass was formerly the site of commercial buildings and residences.

The breakwater in the bay was built to provide a safe port for the town. Construction was started in 1908 and completed in 1929. Approximately 951,273 tons of rock quarried on this island were used to build a barrier that would provide a calm harbor.

Retrace your steps to Furneaux Lane and Kamehameha Avenue. You are now standing across from the **10. Vana Building**, which was influenced by the architecture of countries with warm climates. Notice the red tile roof, arched windows and decorative trim, which add interest to the concrete and wood structure.

Continue walking down Kamehameha Avenue until you come to the **11. S. P. Kress Building**. Your best view of the entire front of the building will be from across the parking area. This building must have left quite an impression on the residents of Hilo when it opened in 1932. Floral designs, batwing shapes and the terra cotta front contributed to introducing a new kind of architecture - art deco.

Return to the sidewalk and continue your walk along Kamehameha Avenue until you come to Kalakaua Street. From the corner you can look across to the **12. First Hawaiian Bank Building**. This sturdy concrete building with its parapet, fluted columns and wrought iron design in the window above the doorway was built in 1930. This is another example of a building by the famous Hawaii architect C. W. Dickey. it survived both the 1946 and 1960 tsunamis.

Walk a little farther along Kamehameha Avenue and stop before crossing Waianuenue Avenue. Look across the street at **13. Koehnen's, Inc.** The blue of the building immediately catches your eye. It is built of reinforced concrete in an adapted version of Renaissance revival style. The recently remodeled exterior emphasizes the decorative details of the building. Originally built for the Hackfield Company in 1910, it was later purchased by Amfac. The Koehnen family bought the building in 1957. The interior walls are made from koa and the floors are ohia.

Cross Waianuenue Avenue and look toward the ocean. Between 1863 and 1890 a number of landing wharves were built at the foot of **14. Waianuenue Avenue**. Passengers and freight were transported by whale boats or lighters between the wharf and steamers anchored in the bay. If the bay was too rough, unloading was done on the beach. In the early 1900s the community agreed to have a wharf built at the Waiakea end of Hilo Bay where the waters were calmer.

 WALK 21 - HILO SCENIC WALK   2 miles
45 minutes

Start this walk near the Hukilau Seaside on Banyan Drive. As you walk along Banyan Drive, on your right you'll see Reed's

Bay, a scenic spot filled with boats. The bay was named after William Reed, a prominent Big Island businessman who died in 1880.

The most outstanding feature along this street is the huge Banyan trees that were planted by the people whose names you'll see on little signs next to the trees. Most of them were planted in the 1930s and dedicated to the City of Hilo.

You'll pass Uncle Billy's Hotel, which has free hula shows at 6:00 p.m. every evening in the restaurant.

Just past the Hilo Hawaiian Hotel, turn right on Lihiwai, and right again where you see the Hawaii Visitors' Bureau warrior sign pointing the way to Coconut Island.

Cross the footbridge and visit the island, which was called Mokuola (healing island) by the early Hawaiians. It used to be visited by those seeking cures for diseases. The waters surrounding the island were believed to have healing properties. The island was also a pu'uhonua, or place of refuge, where lawbreakers could find forgiveness.

Coconut Island is a fun place for children. It has a sheltered

Liliuokalani Garden (Photo courtesy of Hawaii Visitors Bureau)

swimming cove, restrooms and picnic tables.

Backtrack to Lihiwai Street and cross the street to visit Liliuokalani Gardens, a lovely 30-acre oasis that is the largest formal oriental garden outside Japan. It was named after Hawaii's last reigning monarch. Explore and discover the stone lanterns, bridges, bamboo, rock gardens and other delights in this tranquil setting.

Linger in the park as long as you like, and then continue walking along Lihiwai Street until you come to the Suisan Fish Market, located where Hwy. 19 crosses the Wailoa River. This place is an interesting beehive of activity about 7:30 a.m., when fish are auctioned here. It's about one mile to this point.

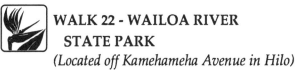

WALK 22 - WAILOA RIVER   .5 miles
STATE PARK   30 minutes
(Located off Kamehameha Avenue in Hilo)

This scenic park is a fine place to take the family, and offers several points of interest.

Park at the Wailoa Center parking lot and start with the Center's exhibition room, where they feature changing art exhibits. The Center is open Mondays, Tuesdays, Thursdays, and Fridays from 8:00 a.m. to 4:30 p.m., Wednesdays from noon to 8:00 p.m. and Saturdays from 9:00 a.m. to 3:00 p.m. The Center also has an information desk with visitor information.

Downstairs take a look at the historic photos of the devastation caused to Hilo by the tsunami (tidal waves) of 1946 and 1960.

In front of the Center you'll notice the new Vietnam Memorial, which was erected in 1988. Behind the Center, take a look at the Shinmachi Tsunami Memorial.

The Wailoa River, the State's shortest river, flows into the Park and meets the Waiakea Fishpond. This is an especially scenic area to walk. Walk across the footbridges and follow the path around the fishpond, where you can go fishing, have a picnic, or watch the ducks cavort. The palms, pandanus and poinciana trees help create a lovely tropical setting here.

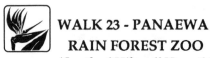

WALK 23 - PANAEWA RAIN FOREST ZOO

(South of Hilo, off Hwy. 11 on Mamaki St.)

12 acres
30-45 minutes

This 12-acre animal park receives over 125 inches of rain a year and is the only rainforest zoo in the U.S.. It opened in 1977 and contains an interesting collection of plants and animals found in the rainforests of the world.

The zoo contains 151 animals, including 11 that are on the endangered list. For a look at some unusual creatures, check out the anteater, pygmy hippos and the Hawaiian hawk. For an added treat, coordinate your visit with the zoo's feeding times of 9:00 a.m. and 3:15 p.m. The zoo also features a botanical garden with both native and introduced species.

The zoo is open daily from 9:00 a.m. to 4:00 p.m., and there is no admission charge. You can walk through the park in 30 to 45 minutes, but you'll want to spend more time enjoying the sights. There are also picnic facilities.

WALK 24 - AKAKA FALLS

(At Honomu on Hwy. 19 turn on Hwy. 220 and drive about 4 miles to a parking area for Akaka Falls State Park.)

.5 miles
30 minutes

There's a loop trail through a lush rainforest filled with ginger, plumeria, banana trees, bird of paradise and ferns. You'll encounter two falls along the way, Kahuna and Akaka, a 424-foot waterfall that is the longest in Hawaii.

The waterfalls are spectacular, and the flora of the rainforest is diverse and fascinating. The dense vegetation here makes this an especially delightful walk. The walk takes about 30 minutes and is easy enough for almost everyone.

There are picnic and restroom facilities in the park, so pack a lunch and stay awhile.

Kona

WALK 25 - HISTORIC KAILUA-KONA

1 mile, one way
30 minutes

Begin this walk at the Hotel King Kamehameha at the end of Ali'i Drive. Beside the hotel is the reconstructed heiau (temple) Ahuena, which is part of the compound known as **Kamakahonu**, where King Kamehameha spent his last days. This compound is a National Historic Landmark. (See Guided Walks, page

Across from the compound is the **Kailua Pier**, which is the heart of much of the fishing and recreational activity in Kailua-Kona. If you walk along here in the late afternoon, you can watch the fishing boats return with their daily catch. This is also the site of the world-famous Hawaii International Billfish Tournament, which is held each summer.

Walk along Ali'i Drive on the ocean side until you come to the Hulihe'e Palace, built in 1838 by former Governor Kuakini. After his death in 1894 Hulihe'e became the summer palace for Hawaiian royalty. It now contains the furnishings of the Hawaiian court and is open daily from 9:00 a.m. to 4:00 p.m. There is an admission charge.

Across the street is the **Mokuaikaua Church**, the oldest in Hawaii, erected in 1837 by the first group of missionaries. The church is built of coral, koa and ohia woods.

Continue walking along Ali'i Drive through the heart of Kailua-Kona's shopping area until you come to **St. Michael's Church**, the first Catholic church built outside of Honolulu, completed in 1840.

Across the street you'll see the new **Waterfront Row** center, which contains shops and restaurants. Go up in their observation tower for an interesting view of the town.

Ali'i Drive continues for about four more miles, and there is a lane along the road for joggers and bikers that makes for easy walking here. If you want to continue, watch for the remains of the **Ohana Church** at the 21/2 mile point. This Congregational church was built in 1895 by Reverend John Paris.

At the 4 mile point you'll reach **Disappearing Sands Beach**, where the sand disappears in the winter, but is brought back in the summer.

This walk can be very hot and sunny, so protect yourself from too much sun.

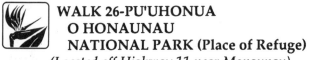

WALK 26-PU'UHONUA O HONAUNAU NATIONAL PARK (Place of Refuge)
(Located off Highway 11 near Monaunau)

.5 miles
30-45 minutes

These ancient grounds provided a place where defeated warriors or anyone else needing protection could come for refuge. Once inside the pu'uhonua (place of refuge), persons were granted asylum and were absolved of any wrongdoing.

At the front desk pick up a brochure, which contains a map and descriptions of all the sites in the 180-acre park. There is a small admission charge.

This site is the last of its type remaining. The Park is administered by the National Park Service, which has attempted to restore the area to its appearance in the late 1700s. Some of the structures date back to the 1500s.

This site was the home of the ruling chief, whose courtyard adjoined the pu'uhonua. The great stone wall, which is still standing, separated the palace grounds from the pu'uhonua. The site also contained three heiau (temples), one of which has been reconstructed.

The path around the park is about 1/2 mile long, and 17 sites are numbered and described in the Park's brochure.

Kohala

| WALK 27 - KALAHUIPUA'A | 2 miles, round trip |
| TRAIL | 1 hour |

Take the Kaahumanu Hwy (19) to Mauna Lani Drive, turn toward the ocean and the **Mauna Lani Resort**. Park near the historic park.

The area known as Kalahuipua'a once belonged to Kamehameha III's queen. It was later purchased by Samuel Parker, grandson of Parker Ranch founder John Palmer Parker.

In 1972 Mauna Lani Resort bought the property, and they have preserved the cultural and historic features of the site. At the Mauna Lani Bay Hotel you can ask at the front desk for their brochure, which includes a map of the trails and a description of the sites.

The Kalahuipua'a trail begins near the parking lot and winds through a historic park that contains several archaeological sites, including lava tube caves, petroglyphs and ancient fishponds. Follow the trail around to the 5-acre Kalahuipua'a fishpond, which is one of the best remaining examples of a traditional Hawaiian fishpond.

To the right is **Keawanui Landing**, which has a replica of a canoe shed housing a full-scale model of an outrigger fishing canoe marking the landing site of King Kamehameha I's canoe landing and village.

To the left, between the fishpond and the ocean is the **Eva Parker Woods Cottage Museum**, which was built in the 1920s and later moved to this site. The cottage houses an exhibit offering a glimpse into the lives of Kalahuipua'a's earliest inhabitants.

Follow the walkway across the bridge that leads to the "sleep house" on a tiny island in the pond, and then return to the trail that follows the shoreline. The Ala Kahakai Shoreline trail is part of an extensive foot trail that connected ancient villages along the Kona-Kohala coast.

Following the trail on around to Honoka'ope Bay will lead you past several scenic spots and ancient archaeological sites.

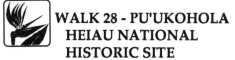

WALK 28 - PU'UKOHOLA HEIAU NATIONAL HISTORIC SITE

1 mile
30 minutes

(Located off Highway 270 near Kawaihae)

This 77-acre National Park contains the sites of three ancient heiau (temples).

Start at the Visitor's Center and pick up a brochure, which contains a map and a description of the grounds. The Park Ranger will also give you a brief orientation to the park. The trail around the park is about one mile roundtrip.

The most famous heiau on this site is Pu'ukohola ("hill of the whale"), completed in 1791 by Kamehameha I. He supposedly built this temple because a prophet told him that if he did so, he would conquer all the Hawaiian Islands. He built the temple, dedicated it to his war god, Ku-Kailimoku, and four years later became the ruler of all the Hawaiian Islands.

Pu'ukohola was the last major religious structure built by the ancient Hawaiians in the Islands. It was used from 1791 to 1819 and housed an altar, wooden images of Hawaiian gods, a prayer tower and thatched houses.

The second site you'll come to is Mailekini heiau. Offshore is believed to be the site of the third heiau, Hale-o-ka-puni. The next point of interest is Pelekane, the site of Kamehameha's residence.

Cross over Highway 270 to visit the site of the house of John Young, a British sailor who was stranded in Hawaii in 1790. He served as an advisor to Kamehameha, and became governor of the Island of Hawaii from 1802 to 1812. His house was probably the first western-style house in the islands.

Archeological work is continuing at the park, and visitors should be careful to help preserve this historic treasure.

Kalopa Native Forest State Park (Photo courtesy of County of Hawaii)

Honokaa

WALK 29 - KALOPA NATIVE   .7 miles
FOREST STATE PARK   **30 minutes**
(Located 5 miles from Honokaa off Highway 19)

This delightful State Park is situated at a 2,000-foot elevation in a native rain forest. There is an easy .7-mile loop trail through ancient ohia trees and a variety of other endemic plants. The whole Kalopa forest consists of 615 acres, of which 100 acres were set aside as a State Park.

There is also a 4-acre arboretum, which was established in 1976 with plants that do not grow naturally in the park, but are found elsewhere on the Big Island. One section is reserved for Polynesian introductions.

The native forest is also home to the *'io* (Hawaiian hawk), the *'elepaio* (flycatcher) and the *'auku'u* (night heron). In a 1972 vegetation survey, 26 species of native trees, shrubs and vines were identified in the rain forest.

The trail starts near the parking area, and here you can pick up a brochure with a map and descriptions of many of the plants you'll see along the trail. If you're inclined to explore the park further, there are other trails through the forest listed in the brochure.

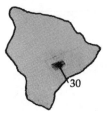

Volcano

WALK 30 - HAWAII VOLCANOES NATIONAL PARK

1 mile
45 minutes

A fascinating area to explore is Hawaii Volcanoes National Park. It's an all day adventure, but the park contains several short walks that will appeal to the whole family. There are also more lengthy and strenuous walks for those inclined to explore the park more thoroughly. There is an admission charge to enter the park.

Take Highway 11 into the park, and the Ranger will give you a map and brochures about the area. Stop first at the Visitor Center, which is open from 7:45 a.m. to 5:00 p.m. daily and offers informative displays and presentations about the geology and cultural history of Hawaii.

Next door to the Visitor Center is the Volcano Art Center, which has an impressive selection of arts and crafts by local artists.

The volcanic eruption of Kilauea in the Hawaii Volcanoes National Park. (Photo courtesy of Hawaii Visitors Bureau)

Follow the signs to Volcano House, which surely must be the only hotel in the world perched on the rim of a volcanic crater. An observation deck at the back of Volcano House provides a stunning view of Kilauea Crater. In front of the hotel the pathway leads you through an area of local trees that are labeled for visitors.

To visit the next site, the Thurston Lava Tube, you can walk or drive, following the signs to the lava tube parking area. A sign points out the beginning of the 1/2-mile loop trail which passes several spots offering excellent views of Kilauea Iki Crater.

The trail will lead you into a 25-acre rain forest that is home to many rare Hawaiian birds, native ferns, ohia and other plants. The trail soon enters a prehistoric lava tube that was discovered in 1913 by Lorrin Thurston, a local newspaper publisher. The tube has lights, but watch your head and look out for water puddles. Follow the trail, which loops back to where you started.

Other short walks are Devastation Trail, Sulphur Banks Trail and the Sandalwood Trail. Signs near the Visitor Center point the way to where the trails begin. Check your Park map for more details.

Another interesting short walk that can be done during a one-day visit to the park is the Kipuka Puaulu (Bird Park).

As you leave the Visitor Center and exit the park past the Ranger's booth, turn left on Highway 11 heading toward Kona. Turn right on Mauna Loa Road and follow the signs to Kipuka Puaulu (Bird Park). A kipuka is an island of land that was surrounded by fast-flowing lava but was left untouched. This 100-acre kipuka contains one of the richest concentrations of native plants in Hawaii.

Sometimes there are brochures at the trailhead that describe the flora and fauna, or you can request one at the Visitor Center. The trail is one mile long, and takes about an hour. It loops through forest and meadow, and there are plant markers along the way. The trail is easy to follow and brings you back where you started.

Island of Maui

West Maui/ Lahaina

| WALK 31 - HISTORIC LAHAINA | 1.5 miles, round trip
1 hour |

1. The **Masters' Reading Room** at the corner of Front and Dickenson was restored by the Lahaina Restoration Foundation in 1970. Originally a storeroom for the missionaries, whaling ship captains converted it to a downtown "officers' club," in 1834. It now serves as the headquarters of the Lahaina Restoration Foundation. Its unique, coral block and fieldstone construction has been preserved exactly as originally built.

2. The two-story **Baldwin Home** was the home of the Protestant medical missionary Dwight Baldwin and his family from the mid-1830s to 1868. The house served as a medical office, and as a general center for missionary activity, with a seamen's chapel and Christian reading rooms. The Baldwins had a fine garden of native and introduced plants: kukui, kou, banana, guava, figs, and grape arbors. The home and grounds were restored by the Lahaina Restoration Foundation in the early 1960s, complete with many pieces of original furniture and other antiques of the period. The museum is open daily, and there is an admission charge.

3. William Richards was the first Protestant missionary to arrive in Lahaina, and the **Richards House** was the first coral stone house in the islands. Richards left the mission in the mid-1830s to work directly for the kingdom as chaplain, teacher, and translator to Kamehameha III. He helped draw up the constitution, traveled to the United States and Europe as the king's envoy, and served as the first Minister of Education. He eventually retired to New England, where he died in 1897. His body was returned for burial in the Waine'e Churchyard **(18)**.

4. The remnants of a substantial **Taro Patch**, called Kapukaiao, were visible as late as the 1950s. Kamehameha III is said to have worked there to show his subjects the dignity of labor.

Located in the Lahaina Harbor, the *Carthaginian II*, a replica of a 19th century brig, is a floating museum containing exhibits on the early history of whaling.

(Photo courtesy of Hawaii Visitors Bureau)

5. The **Hauola Stone** is popularly believed to have been used by the Hawaiians as a healing place.

6. The **"Brick Palace,"** built around the year 1800 by two ex-convicts from the British penal colony at Botany Bay, Australia, was almost certainly the first western building in the islands. It was made of locally-produced brick. Constructed at the command of Kamehameha I, it was used intermittently as a storehouse and a residence until the 1850s. The cornerstones and foundations have been excavated, and a display built by the Lahaina Restoration Foundation for the Maui County Historic Commission.

7. The *Carthaginian* is a replica of a 19th century brig, typical of the small, fast freighters that brought the first commerce to the Sandwich Isles. Authentically square-rigged, the ship features an exhibit on whales and whaling with colorful audio-visual displays and an original whaleboat discovered in Alaska and returned to Lahaina in 1973. The museum is open daily, and there is an admission charge.

8. The **Pioneer Inn**'s original section, fronting the harbor, dates from 1901. Additional rooms and shops were added in 1965, but this extension was carefully built to match the style of the original. It served as the only visitor accommodation in West Maui until the late 1950s. The stern turn-of-the-century regulations for guests are still posted in the rooms.

9. The **Banyan Tree**, more than sixty feet high and casting shade on two-thirds of an acre, was planted in 1873 to mark the fiftieth anniversary of the beginning of Protestant missionary work in Lahaina.

10. The **Courthouse** was built with stones from the demolished Hale Piula. It served as a customhouse as well, and was the center of anti-smuggling activity during the whaling era. Here in August, 1898, the Hawaiian flag was lowered and the American flag raised, marking the formal annexation of the islands by the United States.

11. The reconstructed remains of part of the waterfront **fort** stand in the corner of Banyan Park. The fort was built in the early 1830s after some sailors lobbed cannonballs at the town during an argument with Protestant missionaries over the visits of native women to ships. Visitors thought the fort looked as if it were built more for show than force. It was used mostly as a prison, and was torn down in the 1850s to supply stones for the construction of Hale Pa'ahao **(21)**.

12. Lahaina had no natural harbor like Honolulu's, only an open roadstead, and the whalers' small "chase boats" had to come in from the deep-water offshore anchorage to trade. When the surf was up, they often had trouble beaching. In the early 1840s, the U. S. consular representative dug a **canal** to a basin near the market, and charged a fee for its use. After a few years, the government took over the canal and built a thatched market house with stalls - which almost immediately burned down. The canal was filled up in 1913.

13. At the **Government Market,** all trade between natives and ships was carried on. "These are the things which I strictly forbid," ran the edict of Princess Nahi'ena'ena in 1833, "overcharging, under-selling ... wrangling, breaking of bargains, enticing, pursuing, chasing a boat, greediness ... I hereby forbid women from going to the market enclosure, for the purpose of sightseeing or to stand idly by ...." Despite this, the area around the market was noted for its gamy activities, and was called Rotten Row.

14. The **Episcopal Church** in the islands was founded in 1862. The present building dates from 1927 and is notable for an altar painting depicting a Hawaiian Madonna and colorful endemic plants and birds.

15. Hale Piula, "iron-roof house," a large two-story stone building with a surrounding piazza, was built in the late 1830s as a palace for Kamehameha III. It was not a success. In fact, it was never finished. The king preferred to sleep in a small thatched hut nearby. By the mid-1840s, the king and his advisers were spending more time at Honolulu than Lahaina, and Hale Piula fell into disrepair. It was used as a courthouse for some time, and after a gale damaged it badly in 1858, its stones were used to build the present courthouse **(10)**.

16. The bland, flat surface of **Maluuluolele Park** hides one of the most interesting parts of old Lahaina. Once there was a pond here, called Mokuhinia, which was believed to be the home of a powerful water spirit in the form of a lizard or dragon. A tiny island in the pond, Mokuula, was for decades a home of Maui chiefs, and then a residence of three Kamehameha kings. Several important chiefs of the early 1800s were buried there. Kamehameha III used to receive visitors at the royal tomb in the late 1830s and early 1840s, showing them the large burial chamber, with its mirrors, velvet draperies, chairs, kahili (feathered staffs), and ornate coffins. In 1918, long after the chiefs' remains were removed, the pond was filled and the island leveled.

17. Waine'e Church was the first stone church in the islands, built for the Protestant mission between 1828 and 1832 by natives under the direction of their chiefs. It could seat 3,000 Hawaiians packed together on the floor and had calabash spittoons for tobacco-chewing chiefs and ships' masters. A whirlwind unroofed the church and blew down the belfry in 1858; the bell, once described as "none too sonorous," fell a hundred feet undamaged. In 1894, native royalists protesting the annexation of Hawaii by the U.S. burned the church. Rebuilt, it burned down again in 1947, was rebuilt, and was demolished by another whirlwind in 1951. The new church, dedicated in 1953, was renamed Waiola, "Water of Life."

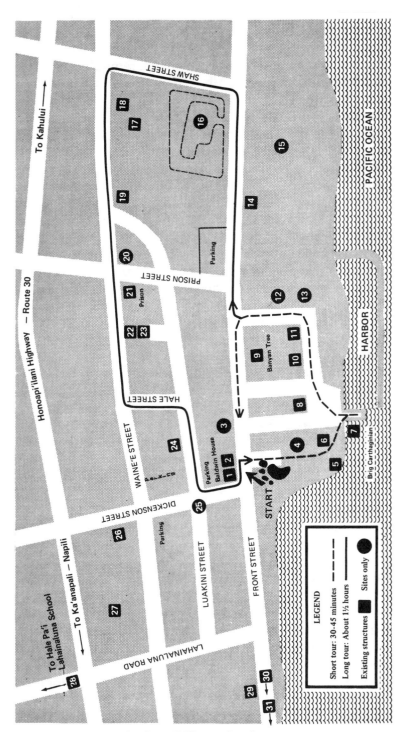

Lahaina Historical Map

18. Waine'e Churchyard. Here are buried the great and obscure of early Lahaina - Hawaiian chiefs and commoners, seamen, missionaries. Here and there are reminders of the old custom of marking the tomb with a glass-framed picture. Among the stones are those of Governor Hoapili and his wife Kalakua; Ke'opuolani, wife of Kamehameha I and mother of Kamehameha II, Kamehameha III, and Princess Nahi'ena'ena; and pioneer missionary William Richards (3).

19. Members of the Buddhist **Hongwanji Mission** have been meeting here since 1910, when they put up a small temple and a language school. The present building dates from 1927.

20. David Malo's House was near the junction of Prison Road and Waine'e Street. Malo, educated at Lahainaluna Seminary as an adult, was the first renowned Hawaiian scholar and philosopher. He developed a keen sense of judgment and was a prime mover in framing the bill of rights and the constitution. His account of the ancient culture, *Hawaiian Antiquities*, has become a classic. Bitter about growing white control of Hawaii, he asked to be buried above the tide of the foreign invasion, and his grave site is on the top of Mt. Ball, above the school. David Malo Day is celebrated annually at the high school in late spring.

21. Hale Pa'ahao, "stuck-in-irons-house," was Lahaina's prison from the 1850s. Built at a leisurely pace by convict laborers out of coral stone from the demolished waterfront fort (11), it had the standard wall shackles and ball and chain restraints for difficult prisoners. Most of the inmates were there for desertion from ships, drunkenness, working on the Sabbath, or dangerous horse-riding.

22. The **Episcopal Cemetery** on Waine'e Street contains burial sites of many early families on Maui who joined the Anglican Church after the Archbishop of Canterbury in England was specifically requested to form a church in Hawaii by Queen Emma.

23. Hale Aloha can be seen from the cemetery. The "House of Love" was built by native Protestants in "commemoration of God's causing Lahaina to escape the smallpox, while it desolated Oahu in 1853, carrying off 5-6,000 of its population." Completed in 1858, it was used as a church and school for many years, but by the early 1900s it fell into ruins. The County of Maui restored the structure in 1974.

24. The **Buddhist Church of the Shingon Sect,** with its green paint and simple wooden architectural style, is typical of church buildings put up all over Maui in the plantation era, when Japanese laborers were imported to work in the sugar fields.

25. Along **Luakini Street** in 1837 passed the funeral procession of the tragic Princess Nahi'ena'ena. Caught between the ancient and the modern world, she alternately worshipped the Protestant God, and yearned after the old traditions, in which a union with her brother Kamehameha III would have preserved the purity of the royal family. She had a son by the king in August 1836. The boy lived only a few hours, and Nahi'ena'ena herself died in December. She was twenty-one. Along the way to her burial place, a path was made through stands of breadfruit and koa trees. It became known as Luakini Street, after the Hawaiian word for the sacrificial heiau, the state temples of the old religion.

26. Maria Lanakila Church, on Dickenson Street near Waine'e Street. The first Roman Catholic mass was celebrated on Maui in 1841, and there has been a Catholic church on this site since 1846. The present church, a concrete replica of an earlier structure, dates from 1928.

27. The **Seamen's Cemetery** on Waine'e Street. Herman Melville's cousin was buried here, as well as one of Melville's shipmates who died in the Seamen's Hospital of a "disreputable disease." Over the years, the marked graves of sailors gradually disappeared, until now only one or two are identifiable.

28. The **Wo Hing Temple** on Front Street is affiliated with the Chee Kung Tong, a Chinese fraternal society with branches all over the world. This one dates from early in this century, when the local society had over a hundred members. The Chinese were among the earliest immigrants to Hawaii and became a powerful force in the commerce of Lahaina. There is an admission charge to the temple.

(Reprinted from "Lahaina: A Walking Tour of Historic and Cultural Sites," with permission of the Lahaina Restoration Foundation)

WALK 32 - KAANAPALI BEACH

2 miles
45 minutes

   Begin this walk behind the Sheraton Hotel, where you'll notice the most outstanding geological feature of the area, a volcanic cinder cone named Pu'u Keka'a (the rumbling hill), which is known locally as Black Rock.

   In Hawaiian tradition, Pu'u Keka'a was known as a *leina a ka 'uhane*, or "soul's leap." When a person was ready to die, the soul would leave the body and go to Pu'u Keka'a. If all earthly obligations had been fulfilled, the soul would be taken by the gods. Each island had at least one *leina a ka 'uhane*.

   This area was also the home of Chief Kaka'alaneo, who ruled West Maui.

   Prior to World War II, the Kaanapali area was owned by the Pioneer Mill Company, which cultivated sugar cane in the area and used Black Rock as a landing site to ship the processed sugar. The ruins of Kaanapali Landing are still visible on the right side of Black Rock.

   Construction of the hotels here began in the early 1960s.

   Kaanapali Beach begins at the ruins of the old Kaanapali Landing and runs for over a mile toward Honokowai Beach Park, where you'll find restroom, shower and picnic facilities.

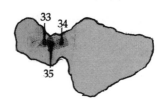

Central Maui/ Wailuku

WALK 33 - IAO NEEDLE
(West Main Street in Wailuku becomes Iao Valley Road and leads to the Iao Needle parking area.)

.5 miles
20 minutes

   This is Maui's most visited attraction, so don't leave valuables in the car.

   There's a paved walkway that crosses Iao Stream and goes up

Iao Needle (Photo courtesy of Hawaii Visitors Bureau)

to a lookout point for viewing the Iao Needle, a 2,250-foot volcanic rock that has survived erosion.

This valley is the oldest part of Maui, and still contains a few ancient heiau and other structures. It's also the site of one of the island's bloodiest battles. In 1790 Kamehameha fought Maui's warriors here and drove them up the stream into the valley. The stream was reportedly dammed by bodies, and the battle was referred to as Kepaniwai (damming of the waters).

You can also walk down by the stream and dip your toes in the cool, fresh water or jump in if you're so inclined. The walk up to the lookout point takes only about 15 to 20 minutes.

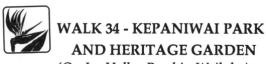

WALK 34 - KEPANIWAI PARK
AND HERITAGE GARDEN
(On Iao Valley Road in Wailuku)

.5 miles
20 minutes

This park is located next to the historic Iao Stream, which reportedly was filled with bodies during the battle of 1790, when Kamehameha the Great slaughtered the greater part of Maui's forces. The battle was called Kepaniwai, which means "the damming of the waters."

The park contains picnic facilities, a small children's swimming pool, and a unique Heritage Garden developed by landscape architect Richard Tongg. Pavilions built in the representative style of the different cultures in Hawaii commemorate the Hawaiians, Japanese, Chinese, Filipinos, Portuguese and the missionaries.

This is a good picnic spot, and can be combined with a visit to the Iao Needle, which is only a couple of miles from the park.

WALK 35 - MAUI ZOOLOGICAL
BOTANICAL GARDENS
(In Wailuku take Kaahumanu Avenue to Kanaloa and turn by the War Memorial Gym. The Maui Zoological and Botanical Garden is on the right a short distance down Kanaloa. There is no parking area, so park along Kanaloa.)

.5 miles
20 minutes

The Zoological and Botanical Garden is small and takes only about 20 minutes to walk through, but it's a fun place for small children. The walk is short, and they'll enjoy the animals. It's also a good picnic spot.

The botanical section of the Garden has several labeled plants. The zoo contains monkeys, donkeys, ducks, goats and a few other animals. It's open daily from 9:00 a.m. to 4:00 p.m., and admission is free.

Haleakala

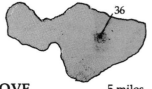

WALK 36 - HOSMER GROVE NATURE TRAIL

.5 miles
30 minutes

(This walk is inside the Haleakala National Park, and there is an admission charge to enter the park.)

At the entrance the ranger will give you a brochure, which includes a map. Right past the entrance there is a sign pointing the way to Hosmer Grove, which has a small parking lot and campground with picnic tables.

At the beginning of the trail there are brochures describing many of the plants along the trail. Several of the plants are labeled, and their numbers correspond to descriptions in the brochure.

Hosmer Grove was started as a forestry experiment in 1910 by Ralph Hosmer, who hoped the trees could be harvested for timber and would improve watershed.

The trail is about 1/2 mile long and is easy walking. It loops through a grove full of exotic plants and birds, and then through an area of native shrubland. It's situated at a 7,000-foot elevation, and the weather is frequently cool and rainy.

The camping area is a pleasant place to have a picnic before starting out to explore the rest of the crater area. There are other trails listed in the park brochure that are more lengthy and strenuous.

Paia/Hana

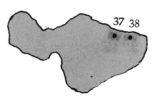

WALK 37 - WAIKAMOI RIDGE TRAIL

.5 miles
20 minutes

(On the road to Hana about 15 miles past Paia)

There is no sign here, but there are usually cars pulled off the road. You'll notice an incongruously placed metal turnstile that marks the beginning of the trail.

The trail is about 1/2 mile long, and takes about 20 to 30 minutes. It loops through a serene forest of bamboo, native ferns, hala trees, large eucalyptus trees, and other introduced species, many with labels. A large sign proclaims "Quiet, Trees at Work."

The trail may be muddy, but it's easy walking, and you'll enjoy the serenity. There is a picnic site which overlooks Kolea Reservoir, a small water containment project.

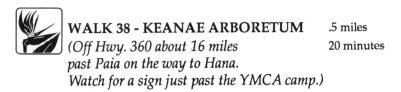

WALK 38 - KEANAE ARBORETUM   .5 miles
(Off Hwy. 360 about 16 miles   20 minutes
past Paia on the way to Hana.
Watch for a sign just past the YMCA camp.)

The arboretum has many labeled plants, both native and introduced, including many cultivated by the ancient Hawaiians. You'll see banana, papaya, sweet potato and many species of taro, a staple of the Hawaiian diet.

There's an easy walk through the arboretum ,ending at taro fields displaying many varieties of taro. There is a trail beyond the taro field, but it's not easy to follow and can be quite muddy. It's best to stop when you get to the end of the taro field and take a splash in the Piinaau stream, which runs through the arboretum.

Island of Kauai

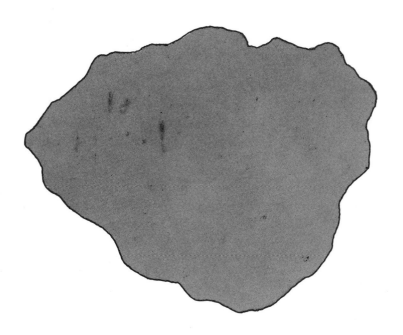

Lihue

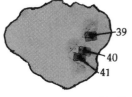

WALK 39 - KILOHANA
(On Hwy. 50 just outside Lihue)

.5 miles
20 minutes

Kilohana is an old plantation estate that has been restored to its original elegance of 1935. The home was built by Gaylord and Ethel Wilcox of Grove Farm Plantation, one of Kauai's largest sugar growers. The 15,000-square-foot house sits on 35 acres of beautiful grounds, which include a tropical garden and a century-old plantation village. There's also an ongoing schedule of cultural events, such as hula performances, Hawaiian crafts and exhibits of local arts.

The house contains memorabilia of the 1930s, including old photos, drawings and antiques. The estate also houses several shops and a restaurant in a picturesque courtyard setting.

You can walk through the house and around the grounds, and there is no admission charge. Kilohana opens at 9:00 a.m. daily.

WALK 40 - KEAHUA ARBORETUM
(Take Route 580 off Hwy. 56
for about 6.8 miles. There's a sign
marking the arboretum.)

8 acres
30 minutes

There is a trail into the arboretum, but it disappears soon, so just explore wherever you'd like. The 8-acre arboretum contains several exotic and native plants, including eucalyptus, monkeypod, kukui, ohia lehua and even a few plants endemic to Kauai.

This is a cool, pleasant spot to bring kids for a picnic. There's a large grassy area for them to run around in, and there's a stream to splash in. Part of the fun of exploring the arboretum is seeing what botanical surprises you can find. During the summer there's an abundant supply of strawberry guavas and wild ginger.

The State is in the process of expanding the arboretum, and is clearing an area for the planting of new trees.

 WALK 41 - LYDGATE PARK
(Off Hwy. 56 at Leho Rd. near theWailua
River. Watch for the "Lydgate Park" sign.)

.5 miles
20 minutes

This beach offers an excellent place to walk and view the sunrise or sunset. The 40-acre park contains a historic site at the north end of the beach. The Hikina A Ka La (rising of the sun) heiau is believed to have been built around 800 A.D. on the first spot in the Wailua area where the rays of the rising sun touch each day.

Next to the heiau is a plaque marking the site of Hauola, one of two ancient places of refuge on Kauai.

A walk along the beach takes you to the mouth of the Wailua River. There are lava pools for wading, but don't attempt crossing the river where it empties into the bay.

Lydgate Park was named after Reverend J. M. Lydgate, who founded the Lihue Union Church over 100 years ago. The park contains restroom and shower facilities, and is a great place for a family outing.

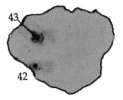

Waimea

 WALK 42 - HISTORIC WAIMEA

2.5 miles
1 hour

1. Begin this walk at the **Russian Fort** (Fort Elizabeth) on Hwy. 50 in Waimea. This fort was built in 1816 by Georg Anton Schaeffer. He was employed by the Russian Fur Company of Alaska, and attempted to persuade King Kaumualii to turn over Kauai to Russia. Schaeffer also built the fort on Oahu near the Aloha Tower that gave Fort Street its name.

Sometimes there are brochures available at the fort entrance.

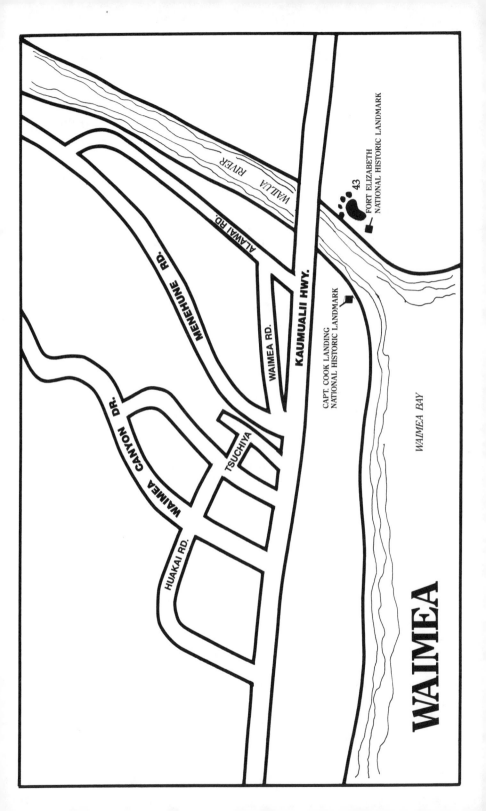

WAIMEA

WAILUA RIVER

FORT ELIZABETH
NATIONAL HISTORIC LANDMARK

43

CAPT. COOK LANDING
NATIONAL HISTORIC LANDMARK

WAIMEA BAY

ALAWAI RD.

WAIMEA RD.

KAUMUALII HWY.

MENEHUNE RD.

WAIMEA CANYON DR.

TSUCHIYA

HUAKAI RD.

The site is a National Historic Landmark, and is maintained by the State.

2. After exploring what's left of the fort, look across the river to see the first landing site of Captain James Cook in 1778. There's a commemorative plaque set in a large boulder near the mouth of the river in **Lucy Wright Park.** For a closer look, walk to the road and cross the bridge over Waimea River.

3. Cross Hwy. 50, walk up Alawai Road and turn left at **Waimea Road.** This street was the original highway and main street into Waimea. Waimea is where the first missionaries to Kauai arrived in 1820.

4. On the left you'll pass the **Waimea Company,** a barn-like building built in 1890. During the depression this was a dance hall.

5. Next on the left is the **First Hawaiian Bank,** built in 1929. This handsome building, built in the neoclassical style, was the only bank on Kauai for many years.

6. The triangular park across the road is the site of the **Captain Cook** statue, placed in Waimea to commemorate the 200th anniversary of Cook's discovery of the Hawaiian Islands.

7. On the right, across from the park, is one of the older buildings, **Hong Min Hee's,** built in 1880 of hand-hewn Hawaiian logs. It now houses Da Booze Shop.

8. Turning right at Ola Road, you'll pass two historical buildings: the **Waimea Educational Community Center,** built in 1933 as a WPA project, and **9.** the **Waimea Christian Church,** also built in 1933, but moved to this site in 1949 after a flood of its previous site near the river.

10. Turn left on Tsuchiya Road, right on Makeke Rd, and left again on Huakai Rd. On your right, you'll see the **Waimea Foreign Church,** built around 1859 by the missionary George Rowell. Cut from a quarry a mile away, the sandstone blocks were dragged by mules to this site. There has been a church on this site since 1825, when a thatched church was built for Rev. Samuel Whitney, the first missionary in this area.

11. In the next block you'll see the **Gulick-Rowell House,** sheltered by a huge monkeypod tree. Peter Gulick built the coral block foundation and walls in 1829, and George Rowell finished it with imported lumber in 1846. It is on the register of historic sites, and is considered the finest example of surviving original missionary structures in Hawaii. It displays an outstanding adaptation of New England building practices to the Hawaiian climate.

12. Backtrack down Waimea Canyon Road and cross Hwy. 50. To the right you'll notice the stark remains of the **Waimea Sugar Mill**, built in 1884. Hurricane Iwa just about finished it off in 1982. Next to the mill, Kikiaola Plantation is converting some of the original plantation housing from the 20s and 30s into vacation homes.

13. Walk toward the ocean and turn left. You'll soon come to the **Waimea Pier**, originally built in 1865. This was the main port for early discoverers and whalers for many years, and for inter-island shipping up until recent times. Starting about 1790, Waimea was the center of the sandalwood trade, which by 1824 had wiped out all the sandalwood trees on the island.

14. Back on Hwy. 50, as you walk back toward the fort, the last point of interest you'll pass is the **Waimea Hawaiian Church**, built in 1865 by Rev. George Rowell when he broke away from the established mission over a personal dispute. Sunday services are still conducted here in Hawaiian.

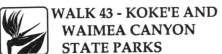 **WALK 43 - KOKE'E AND WAIMEA CANYON STATE PARKS** 1 mile (for trails) 45 minutes half day for park
(From Waimea follow Route 550 to the parking area for Koke'e Lodge.)

Koke'e and Waimea Canyon State Parks cover over 6,000 acres, which include 45 miles of trails. The parks contain many native plants and rare birds, and offer panoramic views of Waimea Canyon and the Na Pali coast. The elevation at the Lodge is around 3,800 feet, and the temperature is about 10 degrees cooler than at sea level.

You should start your explorations at the Koke'e Natural History Museum, which has several displays about the geological features of Kauai. The Museum also has maps of the trails through the park. There is a wonderful green picnic area next to the Lodge, with space for camping.

Two trails that should be easy enough for most people are the Cliff Trail and the Iliau Nature Loop.

Waimea Canyon (Photo courtesy of Hawaii Visitors Bureau)

The Cliff Trail, .1 mile from the end of Halemanu Road, off 550, is an easy walk to a lookout point. There is a sign at the road marking the trailhead.

The Iliau Nature Loop also begins at Route 550 and is marked by a sign at the trailhead. The trail is 1/2 mile long, and has many labeled endemic plants and an excellent view of the canyon. You may also see the iliau plant along the trail. This is a relative of the silversword plant found at Haleakala on Maui.

You should allow at least half a day to drive to and explore Koke'e. It's a good place to picnic, or plan to have lunch at the Lodge.

GUIDED WALKS

ISLAND OF OAHU

1. **Visitors Fitness Walk**. "Pacesetters" Fitness Group for visitors, 7:00 to 9:00 a.m., Mondays, Wednesdays and Fridays, Royal Hawaiian Shopping Center, near McDonald's, 2nd floor. Free. Call 922-0588.

2. **Fitness Walking Program**, Kapiolani Park. Meet at the Bandstand, Sunday mornings at 7:00 a.m. Free. 486-3310.

3. **Reef Walk, Waikiki Aquarium**, 2777 Kalakaua. Discover the creatures of the coral reef with the Aquarium's Education Staff. Both day and night walks are available. Call for dates and times. Fee. 923-9741.

Chinatown:
4. **Chinese Chamber of Commerce** , 42 North King Street. Tuesday mornings at 9:30 a.m. Fee. Reservations recommended. 533-3181.

5. **Hawaii Heritage Center**, 1128 Smith Street, second floor. Wednesdays and Fridays at 9:30 a.m. Fee. 521-2749.

6. **Historic Honolulu**, Mission Houses Museum, 553 South King Street. Monday and Friday at 9:30 a.m. Fee. 531-0481.

7. **Foster Botanical Gardens**, 50 N. Vineyard Street. Mondays, Tuesdays and Wednesdays at 1:30 p.m. Fee.

8. **Lyon Arboretum**, Manoa Valley. First Friday and third Wednesday of the month at 1:00 p.m. and third Saturday at 10:00 a.m. $1.00 donation requested. 988-7378.

9. **East-West Center**, 1777 East-West Rd., University of Hawaii Campus. Meet at Jefferson Hall, Garden level; 1:30 p.m., every Tuesday, Wednesday and Thursday. Free. 944-7691.

10. **University of Hawaii Campus Walk.** Meet at Campus Center forum area on Mondays, Wednesdays and Fridays at 2:00 p.m. for this one-hour walk of the Manoa campus focusing on history, art, architecture and plant life. 948-7235.

11. **Koko Crater Botanical Garden,** inside Koko Crater in Hawaii Kai. Foster Gardens sponsors this walk through a dry land garden. Call for dates and times. Fee. 537-1708.

12. **Moanalua Gardens,** 2850 Moanalua Rd. This 11/2-hour walk is conducted once a month for groups of ten or more, and a $2.00 donation per person is requested. It includes an introduction to the plants, buildings and history of the garden. Call 839-5334.

13. **Bird Walk, Ho'omaluhia Park,** end of Luluku Road in Kaneohe. Observe and learn about Hawaii's birds on this 2-hour walk. Bring binoculars. Call for dates and times. Free. 235-6636.

14. **Hawaiian Ethnobotany Walk,** Ho'omaluhia, end of Luluku Road in Kaneohe. Learn to identify plants used by ancient Hawaiians on this 2-hour walk. Call for dates and times. Free. 235-6636.

15. **Nature Walk, Ho'omaluhia,** end of Luluku Road in Kaneohe. Learn about tropical plants and island natural history on this 2 1/2-hour walk on Saturdays at 10:00 a.m. or Sundays at 12:30 p.m. Free. 235-6636.

Full Moon Walks:
16. **Ho'omaluhia,** end of Luluku Road in Kaneohe. Free. 235-6636.

17.**Waimea Falls Park,** North Shore across from Waimea Bay. Meet at the front entrance at 8:30 p.m. two nights per month during the full moon. Free. 638-8511.

ISLAND OF HAWAII

1. **Historic Hilo,** Lyman Museum, 276 Haili Street, Hilo. Meet at the Museum at 9:00 a.m. the third Saturday of every month. Free.

2. **Ahu'ena Heiau and Kamakahonu Compound,** Hotel King Kamehameha, next to Kailua Pier. Meet in the hotel lobby at 1:30 p.m. Monday through Friday. Free.

3. **Botanical tour,** Hotel King Kamehameha, next to Kailua Pier. Meet in the hotel lobby at 10:30 a.m. on Tuesday or Thursday. Free.

4. **Volcanoes National Park.** Walk through the grounds of Hawaii's oldest heiau ruins and across some of the world's newest lava flows and black sand beaches with a park ranger-naturalist. Call the Kilauea Visitor Center for times. 967-7311.